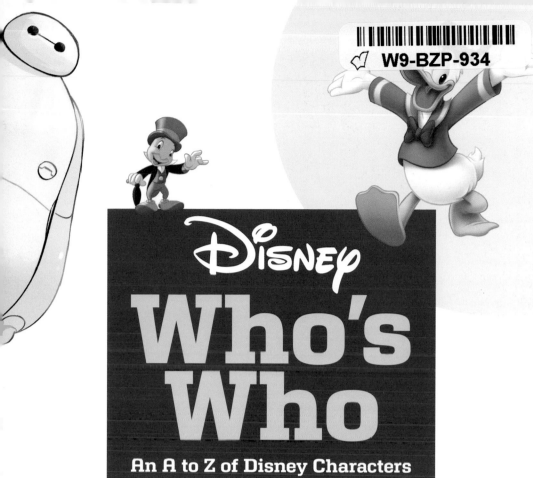

Disney
Who's Who

An A to Z of Disney Characters

Written by
Brooke Vitale

Designed by
Scott Petrower

DISNEP PRESS

LOS ANGELES • NEW YORK

101 Dalmatians is based on the book *The Hundred and One Dalmatians* by Dodie Smith, published by The Viking Press.

The Aristocats is based on the book by Thomas Rowe.

Disney/Pixar elements © Disney/Pixar; rights in underlying vehicles are the property of the following third parties: Hudson, Hudson Hornet, Nash Ambassador, and Plymouth Superbird are trademarks of FCA US LLC; Dodge®, Jeep® and the Jeep® grille design are registered trademarks of FCA US LLC; Petty marks used by permission of Petty Marketing LLC; Mack is a trademark of Mack Trucks, Inc.; Ford Coupe, Mercury, and Model T are trademarks of Ford Motor Company; Porsche is a trademark of Porsche; Sarge's rank insignia design used with the approval of the U.S. Army; Volkswagen trademarks, design patents and copyrights are used with the approval of the owner, Volkswagen AG; FIAT and Topolino are trademarks of FCA Group Marketing S.p.A.; Chevrolet Impala and Corvette are trademarks of General Motors.

The Fox and the Hound is based on the book by Daniel P. Mannix.

The Great Mouse Detective is based on the Basil of Baker Street book series by Eve Titus and Paul Galdone.

Omnidroid © & TM Lucasfilm, Ltd.

The movie *The Princess and the Frog* Copyright © 2009 Disney. Story inspired in part by the book *The Frog Princess* by E. D. Baker Copyright © 2002, published by Bloomsbury Publishing, Inc.

Featuring characters from the Disney films suggested by the books by Margery Sharp, *The Rescuers* and *Miss Bianca*, published by Little, Brown and Company.

MR. POTATO HEAD and MRS. POTATO HEAD are trademarks of Hasbro used with permission. © Hasbro. All rights reserved. Slinky Dog © POOF-Slinky, LLC.

Winnie the Pooh characters are based on the "Winnie the Pooh" works by A. A. Milne and E. H. Shepard.

All illustrations by the Disney Storybook Art Team.

Special thanks to Jean-Paul Orpinas, Jeff Thomas, Brent Ford, Manny Mederos, Jeff Clark, Grace Lee, Scott Tilley, Jenny Spring, Laureen Gleason, Kevin Kern, Dave Smith, Danielle DiMartino, Jennifer Black, Megan Granger, Mariel Pinciotti, Rachel Rivera, Kate Milford, and Jerry Gonzalez.

Printed in the United States of America
Second Paperback Edition, July 2020
10 9 8 7 6 5 4 3 2 1
Library of Congress Control Number: 2019919392
FAC-034274-20150
ISBN 978-1-368-05782-0
Visit www.disneybooks.com

Cruella De Vil

Cruella De Vil lives for fur and cannot imagine life without an enormous collection of it. But Cruella is not content to have just any fur. She wants something truly unique, something no one else has—a Dalmatian fur—and she'll go to any lengths to get it! Cruella has a unique look—black hair on one side of her head and white on the other—and can usually be seen in a yellow fur coat that is several sizes too big for her, making her already thin body seem even smaller. Cruella is reckless, acting more on impulse than premeditation, a fact that leads to her ultimate defeat.

did you **know?**

- **Cruella De Vil was ranked as the American Film Institute's thirty-ninth most evil villain. She also often appears on the Forbes list of wealthiest animated characters.**

Roger Radcliffe

Roger is a songwriter. His goal in life is to create a hit love song. Roger is a bit clumsy and awkward, but he means well and is a good husband to Anita and a good pet to his Dalmatian, Pongo. Although he would never do it to her face, Roger enjoys making fun of Anita's friend Cruella De Vil. He has even written a song about her.

Anita Radcliffe

Anita is the wife of Roger and the pet of a Dalmatian named Perdita. She is also an old school friend of Cruella De Vil's, although she has grown a bit tired of Cruella over the years and has even gone so far as to admit her friend is a bit eccentric. Anita is kind and fun-loving. She enjoys teasing Roger about his songs but is also incredibly supportive. She knows he is a great songwriter, and she has enough confidence for both of them that he will be a star one day.

Pongo

Pongo is a Dalmatian. He and his mate, Perdita, are the proud parents of fifteen Dalmatian puppies and the adoptive parents of an additional eighty-four puppies. Pongo is a romantic. In fact, he is the reason his pet, Roger, is happily married to Anita. If Pongo hadn't taken it upon himself to help Roger find love, they would *both* still be bachelors! Pongo is laid-back, optimistic, playful, and a bit goofy. He and Roger even share their own silly dance, which they perform whenever they have something to celebrate. But Pongo can be serious, too. He has also shown himself to be quite clever and stealthy—traits that helped him rescue his puppies from the evil Cruella De Vil.

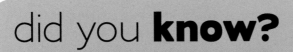

did you **know?**

- **Pongo has seventy-two spots.**
- **Pongo's pet peeve is humans who think they are smarter than dogs.**

Perdita

Perdita is a well-mannered, elegant lady. Unlike her mate, Pongo, who tends to be overly optimistic, Perdita leans toward the negative. She can be very worrisome, with her concern often turning to pessimism. Perdita doesn't handle stress well, preferring to simply avoid hectic, chaotic situations. Her worries aren't always without cause, though, as she seems able to sense danger before it surfaces. In spite of her fears, Perdita is a strong, loving mother. Although a bit of a disciplinarian, she would do anything to protect her puppies and make sure they know they are loved.

Nanny

Originally hired as a cook and housekeeper, Nanny soon becomes caretaker of Pongo and Perdita's puppies. Although technically an employee of the Radcliffes', Nanny is a part of the family. She is overjoyed when the puppies arrive and takes it particularly hard when they are abducted, blaming their kidnapping on herself. Nanny is incredibly loving but also very stern. She does her best to keep the puppies well cared for.

Patch

More than anything, Patch longs to be a hero. He was the only one to fight back when Cruella's henchmen abducted the puppies, and he even stood up to Jasper when the villain spoke harshly to his brother Lucky. Patch looks up to his father as a role model and idolizes Thunderbolt, the dog star of a popular TV show. He has seen and memorized all seventy-two episodes of Thunderbolt's show. Patch has a bit of a rivalry with his brother Lucky. The two are always vying for the best spot in front of the TV. In spite of this, Patch is very protective of Lucky. Patch has one black ear, one white ear, and a black patch around his right eye.

did you **know?**

- **Patch has thirty-two spots. He was the only puppy born with black markings. The others were white at birth and developed black spots later.**

Lucky

Lucky is the weakest of the puppies. He nearly died when he was born, but Roger managed to revive him. He received his name because Roger and Anita felt that he was lucky to be alive. Lucky is shy and soft-spoken. In fact, he is rarely seen speaking to anyone other than Pongo. In spite of his rivalry with Patch, the two are very close. Both idolize Thunderbolt and wish to be like him. Lucky has a horseshoe-shaped pattern on his back and wears a red collar.

Rolly

Mischievous and playful, Rolly is one of Pongo and Perdita's fifteen puppies. The chubby puppy has an incredible sense of smell. He is always hungry and is happy to follow wherever his appetite may lead. Rolly has three spots on each of his ears. Like his brothers, he wears a red collar.

Horace Badun

Horace Badun and his brother, Jasper, are the bumbling thieves hired by Cruella De Vil to kidnap the Dalmatian puppies. Short and fat, Horace loves to eat—particularly sandwiches and cake. In spite of being a bit dim-witted, Horace is rather insightful. He always seems able to correctly guess what Pongo and the puppies are up to and even points out some black Labradors, suggesting perhaps the puppies disguised themselves. Unfortunately for Horace, no one ever seems to think much of his ideas.

Jasper Badun

Jasper is the brains behind the dog-napping—if he can be said to be the brains behind anything! Jasper does not think the Dalmatians are the intelligent animals Horace believes them to be and often underestimates them. Jasper tends to be a bumbling villain. He is also lazy, preferring to play darts and watch *What's My Crime?* on TV rather than care for the puppies he's kidnapped. Jasper is greedy and agrees to do Cruella's bidding for the money, but he is not without a heart. He balks when she suggests he skin the puppies before the police arrive and is ultimately saved from having to do anything truly terrible when the puppies escape.

The Colonel

The Colonel is an Old English sheepdog who lives on a farm in the English countryside with his companions—the Captain, a horse, and Sergeant Tibs, a tabby cat. The Colonel is brave and resourceful. He insists on investigating Cruella's home when he hears that the puppies may be there and is instrumental in rescuing them. The Colonel tends to mishear words, thinking that the Twilight Bark is about "spotted puddles" rather than "spotted puppies." He is also rather forgetful.

Sergeant Tibs

Sergeant Tibs takes his orders from the Colonel. He does as the Colonel tells him, quickly and without question. Like his commander, Tibs is brave and resourceful. Although the Colonel goes with him to investigate Cruella's mansion, it is Tibs who actually goes inside and sneaks the puppies out. In spite of this bravery, Tibs is easily startled. He has also shown a dislike for creepy old houses.

The Peddler

Known simply as the Peddler, this mysterious merchant has a wide assortment of wares to sell, from a coffeemaker that also makes julienne fries to Dead Sea Tupperware. But he is also the holder of the magical lamp and a teller of tales. It is he who shares the tale of Aladdin and the lamp that changed the course of the orphan's life.

Abu

A mischievous monkey with a greedy streak a mile long, Abu is Aladdin's best friend and partner in crime. Unlike Aladdin, who steals to survive, Abu steals simply because he can't help himself. He tries to take anything that grabs his eye, from food to clothes to money. In fact, he and Aladdin met when Abu tried to steal money from Aladdin's pocket! The two have been together ever since. Abu values his friendship with Aladdin above all, and is willing to go to great extremes to ensure Aladdin's happiness. In spite of his many vices, Abu is soft at heart, having shown a willingness to share his stolen goods with those more in need than himself.

Aladdin

Aladdin is a street rat who dreams of having more. Aladdin has been on his own since he was two years old, when his mother was abducted by bandits. Aladdin lives on the streets of Agrabah with his monkey friend, Abu. The two do what they need to survive, which usually means stealing food from street vendors. Aladdin is quick-fingered and fast on his feet. He has to be to stay ahead of the palace guards. Aladdin's world is turned upside down when he is tricked by the Sultan's vizier, the evil Jafar, into stealing a magical lamp. With the help of the Genie in the lamp, Aladdin manages to defeat Jafar and win the heart of Princess Jasmine. These days, Aladdin calls the Sultan's palace home.

did you **know?**

- **Whenever Aladdin (in disguise as Prince Ali) lies, the plume on his hat falls and covers his face.**

- **When disguised as Prince Ali, Aladdin wears shoes. When dressed as himself, Aladdin is always barefoot.**

The Genie

The Genie is one of the most powerful beings in the entire Disney universe. He can shape-shift into almost anything, escape a magically sealed cave, and provide others with great powers, to name just a few abilities. Trapped in his lamp for over ten thousand years, the Genie relishes the opportunity to entertain his masters. He is a showman at heart and will do almost anything for a laugh. He is also an incredibly devoted friend. Although the Genie's body is confined to the lamp, his mind is not. He is capable of seeing into the future and the past. The only thing he cannot see is his own future.

did you **know?**

- **The Genie was designed to look like a living cloud of smoke.**

- **In a deleted concept from *Aladdin*, it was revealed that the Peddler is actually the Genie in disguise.**

- **Many of the Genie's lines were improvised by voice actor Robin Williams.**

- **The Genie's lamp can be seen on Mama Odie's houseboat in *The Princess and the Frog*.**

The Magic Carpet

The Magic Carpet is a sometimes shy, sometimes bold, always clever enchanted object. For thousands of years it lived in the Cave of Wonders—until it was released by Aladdin and Abu. The Magic Carpet is a fiercely loyal friend and a romantic. It saves Aladdin on more than one occasion and even gives him the nudge he needs to kiss Jasmine for the first time. The Carpet is highly intelligent and often seems to understand what is going on before anyone else. Although it is not able to speak, it conveys its emotions in other ways, often using its tassels as hands and feet to act out what it wants to say. The carpet is fond of playing with (and playing tricks on) Abu and beating the Genie at chess.

Rasoul

Rasoul is Agrabah's captain of the guard. He believes in following orders and will do as he's told even when he personally disagrees. Rasoul enjoys being a powerful force in Agrabah, but he is not power-hungry. He simply has no patience for lawbreakers. More than anything, the burly guard just wants to protect his city.

Jasmine

As the daughter of the Sultan and princess of Agrabah, Jasmine leads an isolated life. Her mother died when Jasmine was a child, and her only companions are her father and her pet tiger, Rajah. Although she lives a luxurious life, Jasmine feels suffocated by her circumstances. She longs to be free and see the world, but her status as a princess means she is forbidden from leaving the confines of the palace. Jasmine is fiercely independent, often stubborn, and unafraid to speak her mind, no matter whom she is fighting. But beneath this, she is incredibly compassionate. Jasmine wants to do right by her kingdom and her subjects, just not at the expense of her own freedom.

did you know?

- According to Jasmine, she learned to ride a horse before she learned to walk.

- Although the exact date is not clear, Jasmine's birthday appears to be sometime in February. *Aladdin* takes place shortly before her birthday. When Jasmine and Aladdin take their trip on the Magic Carpet, they fly over China, where Chinese New Year is being celebrated. This holiday is usually observed in February. It can fall anywhere from January 21 to February 20.

Rajah

Rajah is a Bengal tiger and Princess Jasmine's oldest friend. The two have been together since Rajah was a cub. The Sultan gave the tiger to his daughter, who was lonely and in need of a companion. Rajah is fiercely protective of and incredibly loyal to Jasmine. He happily chases away her suitors and even aids in her escape from the palace.

The Sultan

The Sultan is the ruler of Agrabah and Princess Jasmine's father. He is a kind and fair—if rather bumbling—ruler. The Sultan spends the majority of his time ensuring that the laws and traditions of his kingdom are kept up. He lost his wife when Jasmine was young and has since been particularly focused on the law stating that his daughter must marry by the time she turns sixteen. He explains this obsession away by telling Jasmine that he wants to know she will be taken care of, and he tries time and time again to push suitors on her. A bit childish in nature, he finds endless entertainment in shoving crackers into the mouth of Jafar's parrot, Iago, and is easily manipulated and hypnotized by Jafar.

Jafar

Jafar is the royal vizier of Agrabah. He is the Sultan's most trusted adviser and the second-most powerful man in Agrabah. Jafar is also an evil sorcerer. He has spent a lifetime searching for the Cave of Wonders, eager to get his hands on the magic lamp inside so he may become sultan. Jafar is tall, thin, and completely bald, though he usually hides his head under his hat. He carries a staff with the head of a snake, which he uses to hypnotize the Sultan, and is usually accompanied by his parrot, Iago. Jafar's drive for power ultimately backfires when he gets his hands on the lamp and wishes to be a genie, accidentally sentencing himself to a life inside his own magical lamp.

did you **know?**

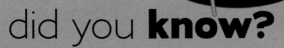

- **It took one year and nine months to record Jafar's lines for *Aladdin*.**

Iago

Iago is the evil sorcerer Jafar's sidekick. Often seen on Jafar's shoulder, the bird is cunning and mischievous. In fact, he is the one who gives Jafar the idea to marry Jasmine to become sultan. Iago is incredibly sarcastic and known to rant when angry. One of his biggest pet peeves is being fed crackers by the Sultan. He gets revenge by shoving crackers into the Sultan's mouth when the Sultan is under Jafar's spell. Iago speaks perfect English, although he hides this ability from everyone but Jafar, and can imitate anyone's voice. He proves this by imitating Jasmine to steal the magic lamp from Aladdin.

Gazeem

Gazeem is one of Agrabah's vilest criminals and Jafar's henchman. On orders of the evil sorcerer, Gazeem tracks down the two halves of a golden scarab, a magical item used to locate the Cave of Wonders. It is Gazeem's job to enter the Cave of Wonders and retrieve the magic lamp. But Gazeem, it seems, is not worthy. When he steps foot inside the Cave, it sinks into the sand, taking the thief with it.

Alice

Alice is a little girl with a *big* imagination. She is also incredibly curious, a trait that leads her to follow the White Rabbit down the rabbit hole and into Wonderland. Having been raised in Victorian England, Alice is incredibly proper and well-spoken. She prides herself on her manners and her honesty, although the two can sometimes be at odds. Alice's attempts to share what she knows often result in her correcting people, which can come across as rude. Her knowledge also isn't of much use in Wonderland, where logic has been turned on its ear. Like her Wonderland rival, the Queen of Hearts, Alice has been shown to have a quick temper. She is, however, far better at reining in her temper and does not stay angry at anyone for long.

did you **know?**

- **Alice most likely comes from a wealthy family, as she references the privileges of the upper class.**

- **Alice's name means "noble" and "kind."**

Dinah

Dinah is Alice's cat and—seemingly—best friend. The two go everywhere together, except to Wonderland. Dinah is tan and peach, with blue eyes and a pink ribbon. She is very fond of chasing mice, a fact that quite startles the Dormouse.

The Cheshire Cat

The mysterious pink-and-purple-striped Cheshire Cat is perhaps the craziest character in all of Wonderland, a fact he admits with pride. He is the only character in Wonderland who shows any real sympathy toward Alice, appearing often to help her find her way. But the Cheshire Cat has a cruel sense of humor and can quickly flop from being helpful to creating accidents that cause the vicious Queen of Hearts to aim her anger at Alice. The Cheshire Cat has the unique ability to appear and disappear at will. But he doesn't do it all at once. The giant smile permanently pasted across his face often lingers in the air long after the rest of his body is gone.

The Mad Hatter

The Mad Hatter lives in Wonderland and can often be found hosting tea parties with his best friend, the March Hare. His favorite occasion to celebrate is his unbirthday, and he is incredibly fond of singing, although he admits he rarely gets compliments on his vocal ability. The hatter seems capable of bending the rules of what a normal person might consider possible, often pouring plates and teacups out of his teapot instead of tea and even making a snack of a plate. He is loud and eccentric, quickly flopping back and forth between happiness and anger, but he can be quite charming as well and takes very quickly to Alice. The hatter is never seen without his signature top hat, which features a card with the numbers 10/6 on it, and under which he has been known to hide any number of items, from a teacup to a present to the sleeping Dormouse!

did you **know?**

- **The 10/6 on the Mad Hatter's top hat is not a fraction but the price of the hat: ten shillings and six pence, in the former currency of Britain.**

- **The Mad Hatter has appeared in an attraction or the name of a shop at every Disney Park in the world.**

The March Hare

Like his best friend, the Mad Hatter, the March Hare is fond of drinking tea and hosting unbirthday parties. He also enjoys polite conversation. Although incredibly loud and often rude himself, the March Hare has no tolerance for rudeness in others. He particularly dislikes being joined by uninvited guests and grows angry when Alice talks before she thinks. In fact, the March Hare is very thoughtful in his own speech, often starting his sentences with a long "Aaaah" as he gathers his thoughts. The March Hare is one of the few residents of Wonderland who doesn't seem to be afraid of the Queen of Hearts, a fact he demonstrates by happily screaming in her face!

The Dormouse

The sleepy Dormouse is a friend to the March Hare and the Mad Hatter. He can usually be found sleeping in one of their teapots, although he has been known to sleep other places, too, like under the Hatter's hat. The dormouse wears a pink coat and bow tie with a purple vest, a white collar, and purple shoes. He is incredibly frightened of cats and has a tendency to sing the song "Twinkle, Twinkle Little Bat." The Dormouse is very fond of jam. Applying it to his nose helps him fall asleep.

The White Rabbit

In spite of displaying a constant fear of being late, the rather jittery White Rabbit is perhaps the sanest resident of Wonderland. He is also the one who leads Alice down the rabbit hole. The White Rabbit is neither polite nor rude. He is simply too busy to notice that Alice, or anyone else, is even around. The White Rabbit works for the Queen of Hearts and is careful to follow her orders closely, for fear of becoming the target of her wrath. When not on duty, the White Rabbit can be seen wearing his signature red coat and carrying his pocket watch. When on duty in the Queen's court, he wears a thick aqua ruffle around his neck and a white flag with a red heart on it.

did you **know?**

- **The White Rabbit explains that his pocket watch was an unbirthday present, but it is not known who gave it to him.**

- **The White Rabbit's watch always reads 12:25.**

The Caterpillar

The Caterpillar is one of the more helpful characters Alice encounters in Wonderland. It is with his help that she learns how to grow bigger and smaller. The Caterpillar has a passion for recitation and grammar, and tends to overenunciate certain words when he speaks. He is one of the calmer residents of Wonderland, but he isn't entirely without a temper. He gets very angry when his height is mocked or when people fail to understand the hints he is giving them. The Caterpillar also seems to be rather forgetful, as he is unable to remember people from one meeting to the next.

Tweedledum and Tweedledee

Tweedledum and Tweedledee are a pair of twin brothers who wear schoolboy uniforms and propeller caps. The two enjoy reciting poems and telling stories. The brothers are playful and jolly, which can sometimes come off as a bit annoying. They enjoy having company and will always try to get their guests to join them for a game. The two also have the ability to multiply.

The Queen of Hearts

The feisty Queen of Hearts is the most dangerous resident of Wonderland. She suffers from immense mood swings, quickly flopping from content to enraged, and her favorite punishment is to behead those who have offended or angered her. The Queen's temper is well known through Wonderland, and she seems to revel in her reputation. She encourages the cheering of the crowds when she orders a beheading and often warns people that if they displease her, they will lose their heads. While the Queen does display a fondness for playing croquet—as long as she doesn't lose—her only true soft spot seems to be for her husband.

did you **know?**

- **Lewis Carroll, the author of the book *Alice in Wonderland*, famously called the Queen of Hearts a "blind and aimless fury."**

- **The Queen of Hearts threatens to have someone's head removed fourteen times during the movie *Alice in Wonderland*!**

The King of Hearts

The soft-spoken King of Hearts is the husband of the Queen of Hearts. He is far smaller than she is and tends to let her rule the kingdom. The King of Hearts's main goal in life seems to be pleasing his wife and keeping her temper at bay. The King doesn't speak up often, so when he does the Queen listens. He is one of the few people in Wonderland capable of calming the Queen down. The King has also shown a particular fondness for trials and likes to see things done in proper order.

The Card Soldiers

The card soldiers are the loyal servants of the Queen of Hearts. They do her bidding without question, possibly because they fear her. When the Queen plays croquet, the cards act as the arches, moving around to ensure the Queen wins the game. The cards also act as guards, escorting the Queen's enemies and prisoners where they need to go. But the cards are not without flaws. They accidentally plant white roses instead of red ones, and then try to hide their mistake by painting the white roses red. It is the card soldiers' hope to fix the problem before the Queen of Hearts finds out and beheads them.

Marie

Marie is a small white Turkish Angora kitten. She and her brothers—Berlioz and Toulouse—live with their mother, Duchess, in Madame Adelaide Bonfamille's home in Paris. Marie prides herself on being a lady. Although she does her best to mimic her mother's behavior, she often comes across as prissy and spoiled. But Marie is not above a good fight and has been known to enjoy a rumble with her brothers from time to time. She is also likely to tattle on them if she does not get her way. Marie is a dreamer, with her head always in the clouds. She also has a beautiful singing voice and is a hopeless romantic. She is the first to welcome Thomas O'Malley to the family as the kittens' new stepfather.

did you **know?**

- **Marie is a middle child. She is also the only female kitten.**

- **Marie starred in her own Japanese music video called "Disney Marie—Walk in Paris."**

- **Marie is named after the French queen Marie Antoinette. In original concept art for the film, she was called Marie Antoinette, but this was later shortened.**

Madame Adelaide Bonfamille

Madame Bonfamille is a wealthy elderly woman living in Paris. She is a retired opera singer and delights in sharing her love of music with her kittens. Madame is kind, friendly, and caring. Having no family and few friends, she dotes endlessly on her cats. She is also incredibly generous. When writing out her will, she leaves the majority of her fortune to her cats. She also creates a foundation that opens her home to the alley cats of Paris.

Duchess

Duchess, a white purebred cat, is elegant and ladylike. She takes being the pet of an aristocrat seriously and is incredibly devoted to Madame. In spite of her upbringing, Duchess is not a snob. She is willing to make friends with anyone, no matter where they are from. Duchess is also a kind, caring mother. She is very protective of her kittens and tries to teach them how to be proper members of French society, even going so far as to teach them to sing and play the piano. But Duchess's compassion has its bounds. She is not a fan of her children's play-fighting and has been known to scold them for it on more than one occasion.

Edgar

Edgar is Madame Bonfamille's butler. Although on the surface he appears to be a polite, sophisticated, honest man, deep down Edgar is actually quite greedy and impatient. When he learns that Madame's fortune is to be left to the cats, he becomes determined to get rid of them. In spite of his behavior, Edgar is not sadistic. His methods for getting rid of Madame's cats may be questionable, but he is careful not to harm them. Ultimately, it is Edgar who disappears, when he is knocked into a box being shipped to Timbuktu.

Berlioz

Berlioz is a small gray kitten with a lighter gray stomach, blue eyes, and a red ribbon tied around his neck. This feisty little cat may seem quiet, but he's actually quite mischievous. Berlioz is hard to impress. He is usually the first to make a snide remark if he sees something he doesn't like, and he is quickly

annoyed. In spite of this, Berlioz is a sweet-natured kitten. He loves to take rides on the head of Madame's horse, Frou-Frou, and is an excellent piano player.

Toulouse

Toulouse longs to meet tough alley cats and tries to pretend to be tough himself. In fact, he can often be seen puffing up his fur to make himself seem bigger. Toulouse has long orange fur and wears a blue ribbon around his neck. In spite of his desire to seem tough, he is actually fairly laid-back and easygoing. Toulouse dreams of being a painter and practices his painting every day.

did you **know?**

• **Toulouse is the oldest of Duchess's kittens.**

Thomas O'Malley

The smooth-talking Thomas O'Malley lives on his own terms. He relishes the freedom of living in the open, with no responsibilities. In fact, the only cats he feels any responsibility toward are his fellow musician friends. But everything changes for O'Malley when he meets Duchess and falls instantly in love with her. Having spent his life on the streets, O'Malley is witty. He puts his wits to good use in saving Duchess and her kittens, and earns himself the home he never knew he wanted with Madame.

did you **know?**

- In the Italian version of *The Aristocats*, O'Malley's name is Romeo.

- O'Malley is referenced in *The Fox and the Hound 2*, when Zelda the cat mentions "a Romeo named Thomas O." she once dated.

Scat Cat

Scat Cat is a musician friend of O'Malley's. Scat Cat is in a band with a group of alley cats. He loves jazz music and is a skilled trumpet player and singer. Scat Cat takes an immediate liking to Duchess and her kittens and is instrumental in rescuing them from Edgar. He ultimately gets adopted by Madame and ends up as a sort of uncle to the three kittens.

The Alley Cats

The Alley Cats are a jazz band that live in a penthouse in Paris with O'Malley. Shun Gon plays the piano, as well as a set of drums made out of pots. Peppo plays the concertina, Billy Bass plays the bass, and Hit Cat plays the acoustic guitar. Their band is rounded out by Scat Cat, who plays the trumpet and sings. The Alley Cats ultimately end up being adopted by Madame Bonfamille when she opens up her home to all the alley cats of Paris.

Roquefort

Roquefort the mouse is a companion of Duchess and her kittens. He lives in a mouse hole in Madame's mansion and often visits with her cats. Although Roquefort is on good terms with Duchess's family, he is quite afraid of other cats. But the little mouse is a brave and devoted friend. When he learns that Edgar plans to ship Duchess and the kittens to Timbuktu, he puts his fear aside to ask Scat Cat and the Alley Cats for help.

Frou-Frou

Frou-Frou is Madame's horse and a dear friend to Duchess and her kittens. She is also Edgar's unwilling confidante, as he confesses to her what he has done to the cats. Frou-Frou is smart and brave. Working with Roquefort, she comes up with a plan to rescue the cats, and in the end, Frou-Frou is Edgar's undoing: she uses her rear hooves to kick him into a trunk bound for Timbuktu.

The Gabble Sisters

Abigail and Amelia Gabble are a pair of British geese encountered by O'Malley and the kittens on their journey back to Paris. The two are twins, distinguishable only by the color of their bonnets. Abigail wears blue while Amelia wears pink. The two are a bit empty-headed and tend to jump to conclusions, but they mean well. They have an uncle named Waldo, who resides in Paris.

Napoleon and Lafayette

This dog duo lives on an abandoned windmill site in the French countryside. Their biggest joy in life is chasing humans who come near their home. Napoleon is clearly the smarter of the two dogs and often gets annoyed at his friend's stupidity. Although he considers himself to be superior to Lafayette, he often takes the smaller dog's advice anyway. As a bloodhound, Napoleon has excellent hearing. He can learn a lot about something just by listening to it. Lafayette, on the other hand, is a bit dopey. He often trips over his large ears and has to lift them with his paw to hear properly. He also speaks before he thinks, and he seems amused by the fact that the pair are repeatedly outsmarted by Edgar.

Milo Thatch

Thirty-two-year-old Milo Thatch has one goal in life: to prove that Atlantis exists and return it to its former glory. Orphaned at a young age, Milo was raised by his grandfather Thaddeus Thatch. Milo graduated from high school at eleven years old and was invited to attend several universities, including Princeton, Harvard, and Yale. He turned them all down in favor of attending Oxford University. In spite of wishing to be an athlete, Milo shows more skill in languages and antiquities. These skills come in handy when an expedition gone awry lands Milo in the very place he's been seeking. Milo ultimately decides to stay in Atlantis. He falls in love with and marries the kingdom's princess and is named king.

did you **know?**

- **Milo is not a fan of carrots.**
- **Milo is the eleventh king of Atlantis.**

Audrey Ramirez

Tough-as-nails Audrey has what her father, master mechanic Manuel Ramirez, refers to as "The Touch." She can pick any lock and fix any machine she encounters. By eighteen months, she could disassemble and reassemble any clock in her house, and by four years old, she could repair a motorcycle on her own. Audrey was born in Detroit. By age nine she was employed at Henry Ford Automotive and was promoted to a managerial position by the age of eleven. Audrey is part of the expedition searching for Atlantis and is instrumental in saving the city. She later returns to the surface, using the gold she receives from the Atlanteans to open a repair shop with her father.

Lyle Tiberius Rourke

Cunning, with an incredibly analytical mind, Rourke has shown a talent for leadership. And it's no wonder. Rourke is simultaneously practical and able to manipulate people to his way of thinking. But beneath his calm demeanor, Rourke is consumed by greed. His goal is to harness the heart of Atlantis to make himself rich. Rourke was expelled from boarding school for fighting and joined the military at the age of fifteen. The ruthless commander has no problem hurting or threatening people to get his way. As a result, he nearly always gets what he wants. Rourke gets more than he bargained for with Milo, who finally bests the bully.

Princess Kida

The daughter of King Kashekim Nedakh, Kida is a warrior princess and fiercely protective of her city. Thousands of years ago, she would not have hesitated to use her combat skills against anyone who trespassed on Atlantean soil. But the years have mellowed Kida, and she has grown curious about the history of her home. Now the inquisitive Kida is more open to visitors, especially if they can help her unlock the secrets of Atlantis. It is this curiosity that allows her to like, and eventually fall in love with, Milo Thatch. Like all Atlanteans, Kida has white hair and dark skin. She also has several blue tattoos. Kida wears a crystal around her neck that allows her to live an extraordinarily long life.

did you **know?**

- **Kida's full name is Kidagakash.**
- **Although Kida appears to be in her early twenties, she is actually over four thousand years old!**

Vincenzo Santorini

Vinny is the demolitions expert on the Atlantis expedition team. Raised in Palermo, Italy, Vinny has had a love for explosives ever since the Chinese laundry next to his family's flower shop blew up. He enjoys creating new explosives, often involving ingredients such as oregano or chili powder, as he feels they make a nice boom. Although Vinny is generally very tough and stoic, he does enjoy playing pranks on Milo. What doesn't he like? Magic, which he calls "hocus-pocus."

Wilhelmina Packard

Over the years, Wilhelmina has held a number of jobs: she has been a dancer, a waitress, and a seamstress, to name a few. But her real passion is communications and creating communications devices. She helped create the Galvanometer, the vibrating telephone, and the Bornite Movable Cup Perkion Detector. Wilhelmina is rather lazy, preferring to do her work when she feels like it, not when she is asked to do it. She has been married at least nine times.

Bambi

Bambi is a young white-tailed deer and a prince of the forest. As a fawn, he is incredibly curious and eager to learn about the world around him. He is also rather clumsy, as he is still learning to get his feet under him. Bambi enjoys playing with his friends, Thumper and Flower, and exploring the woods. He lacks the cautiousness seen in his mother and the other older animals in the forest, and often charges forward without thinking. His status as a prince is important to him, and he is eager to impress his father. By the time he has developed into a mature buck, Bambi is ready to take his rightful place and rule alongside his father, the Great Prince of the Forest.

did you **know?**

- **Bambi makes cameos in several other films, including *The Rescuers* and *Who Framed Roger Rabbit*.**

- **Bambi is so iconic a character for Disney that he even appears on Disney stock certificates.**

Bambi's Mother

Bambi's mother is a kind, protective force. Her job is to shelter and raise her son while her husband, the Great Prince of the Forest, rules over the woods. She takes this task to heart, teaching Bambi all there is to know about the forest and warning him of the dangers of Man. Although her warnings are enough to keep Bambi safe, they are not enough to save her, and she is unfortunately killed by a hunter.

Friend Owl

Friend Owl is known throughout the forest. He is particularly close to the royal family, serving at times as an adviser to the Great Prince. Friend Owl watches over Bambi, offering advice and teaching him about the forest. Although he is usually cheerful, Friend Owl tends to grow grumpy in the spring, as he gets annoyed at all the animals getting twitterpated (his word for falling in love). In spite of this, Owl is quite happy that Bambi finds love with Faline and presides joyously over the birth of their two sons.

43

Faline

A fellow deer, Faline befriends Bambi at a young age. It is she who approaches Bambi at the pond and who later gives him his first kiss. As a young fawn, Faline is sweet, if a bit giggly and bubbly. These traits lessen as she grows up and becomes a more sensible, mature deer. Faline has a tendency to end up in situations where she needs help, whether it is being pursued by an unwanted suitor or chased by hunting dogs. But she is not without resourcefulness of her own. Faline manages to get herself far enough from the hunting dogs to safely await rescue and even escapes from a fire in the forest. Faline ultimately becomes Bambi's mate and the mother to his twin fawns.

The Great Prince of the Forest

Intimidating to look at, The Great Prince of the Forest is truly soft at heart. He is known through the woods for his bravery and wisdom and is said to have lived longer than any other deer in the forest. The Great Prince seems to have an ability to sense oncoming danger, and as such is considered the protector of the forest. Although he is not a big presence in his son's young life, the Great Prince shows little hesitation at taking Bambi under his wing and teaching him the ways of the forest when his mother dies.

Flower

Flower is a little skunk and one of Bambi's best friends. The two meet when Bambi is sniffing the flowers in which Flower is asleep. Bambi is still learning how to speak and mistakenly calls the little skunk "flower," which the skunk allows the fawn to use as his name. Flower is shy and thoughtful. He finds Bambi's many questions charming, although he is not particularly eager to answer them when he is hibernating. Although Flower swears he will not become twitterpated like the other animals in the forest, he cannot help himself. When he matures, he falls in love with a female skunk, and the two have a son whom they name Bambi.

did you **know?**

- **Flower is often mistaken for a girl due to his name and long eyelashes.**

- **Flower's real name is not known, as he agrees to let Bambi call him Flower.**

- **Flower makes a small cameo in *Who Framed Roger Rabbit*.**

Thumper

Thumper is the first and best friend Bambi makes in the forest. Although he is also quite young, Thumper considers himself wise in the ways of the forest and takes it upon himself to teach the young fawn everything he knows. Unfortunately, Thumper's advice, while well-meaning, often gets him and his friends in trouble. Thumper is a playful rabbit. He loves exploring the forest and has an excellent sense of adventure. He also has a good sense of humor, although what he considers to be funny is often perceived by others as mischievous. He is best known for thumping his foot, which is how he claims he got his name.

did you **know?**

- **Thumper has four sisters.**

- **Thumper was originally meant to have a much smaller role in _Bambi_. His part was increased to add comic relief.**

- **According to a line in _Who Framed Roger Rabbit_, Thumper is Roger's uncle.**

- **Thumper is ranked forty-fourth in _Empire_ magazine's "50 Best Animated Movie Characters."**

Cogsworth

Cogsworth runs the Beast's castle. It is his job to keep everything in order and make sure the Beast remains happy. He takes this job seriously, and as such often comes across as rather stern and bossy. Although his desire to abide strictly by the rules often puts him at odds with Lumiere, the two are actually very close friends. Cogsworth is not against having fun. He does, however, try to avoid doing anything that may anger the Beast. Cogsworth is loyal to his master, but his loyalty seems largely tied to fear of the Beast's temper. In spite of this, Cogsworth does display a fondness for the Beast and often takes it upon himself to provide his master with a much-needed ego boost.

Lumiere

This candelabrum is one of the most welcoming enchanted objects in the Beast's castle. He eagerly invites Maurice to seek refuge in the castle and later treats Belle to a fantastic feast—against the orders of his master. Although he clearly cares about the Beast, Lumiere is also rather rebellious. He prefers to do things his own way, no matter what others may think or what orders he may have been given. In spite of this, the Beast often turns to Lumiere for advice, particularly on matters of the heart. Lumiere is in love with the idea of love, although he doesn't seem to fully understand it. He remains more hopeful than most that the Beast will one day find love and that the enchanted objects will be transformed back into humans.

Belle

Despite her beauty, Belle is considered an outsider in her town. Her love of reading and unwavering devotion to her eccentric father, Maurice, make her what the townspeople consider "odd," but that doesn't mean they don't like her. Belle is exceedingly kind. She always has something nice to say and cheerily greets everyone in town each morning. Belle dreams of something bigger than life in her small town. She wants adventure, like those she reads about in her books. Belle also knows what she doesn't want: to be a housewife to the boorish Gaston, no matter how hard he tries to change her mind. In fact, Belle's mind is one thing she is very sure of, and she is not afraid to share her opinion with anyone. Clever and strong-willed, Belle will stand up for herself no matter what. But her status as the town outsider has also taught her to look past what is on the surface and see the best in people, even the seemingly horrible Beast.

did you **know?**

- **Belle is the only main character in her village who wears blue. The animators thought this would accentuate how out of place she is.**

- **Belle's name means "beautiful" in French.**

Maurice

Maurice is generally considered the town kook. The villagers don't understand what drives this eccentric inventor and tend to look down on him. But Maurice doesn't care. He is proud of his inventions and is sure he will someday come up with something that will change his family's life for the better. The only thing Maurice loves more than inventing is his daughter, Belle. Maurice considers Belle to be his greatest accomplishment. He is exceedingly proud of the woman she has grown into and often tells her that she is perfect, no matter what others may say.

Philippe

Belle's trusty horse, Philippe, is really more like a family member than a pet. He seems able to understand Belle when she speaks to him, and it is he who leads her to the Beast's castle to rescue Maurice. But as loyal as Philippe may be to his family, he is also easily frightened, particularly by wolves. He flees the first time he encounters them, leaving Maurice stranded in the woods. When wolves attack him a second time, he bucks, dropping Belle into the snow.

Gaston

Big and brawny, this oversized hunter has an equally oversized ego! He is sure he is better than everyone else, and he's not afraid who knows it. Luckily for Gaston, most of the townspeople seem to agree. Gaston is the town hero. The only person put off by Gaston's arrogance is Belle, the very woman he wishes to marry. Gaston believes that a woman's primary purpose is to have and raise children. He does not believe women should have ideas of their own and particularly frowns on the idea of reading, as it distracts them from more important things—like flattering him! Unfortunately for him, Belle disagrees. This does not sit well with Gaston, who is not used to hearing the word *no*.

did you **know?**

- **Gaston eats five dozen eggs each day. That's around 4,680 calories, just in eggs!**

- **It is unclear whether Gaston is the character's first or last name.**

LeFou

Although he comes across as a bit of a bumbling fool, LeFou is actually quite clever. In fact, it is he who tricks Maurice into telling the villagers about the Beast. In spite of Gaston's negative treatment of him, LeFou is loyal to his friend. He looks up to Gaston as his hero and does as he is told, usually without question. But that doesn't mean LeFou is above making fun of Gaston. He's been known on occasion to laugh at or make snarky comments about his friend, although he usually gets hit by Gaston as a result.

Monsieur D'Arque

Proprietor of the local mental hospital, Asylum de Loons, Monsieur D'Arque is a cold, callous man who seems to take pleasure in other people's pain. He is also driven by greed. In exchange for proper compensation, he happily signs on to Gaston's plan to lock up Maurice in the asylum unless Belle agrees to marry Gaston. Later, Monsieur D'Arque assures Belle that Maurice will be "well taken care of"—but the sinister way he says it implies that his inmates may be subject to some very poor treatment indeed.

The Bimbettes

These identical triplets live in the same village as Belle and work as waitresses in a local tavern. The three are infatuated with Gaston and dream of marrying their hero, even if he barely seems to know they exist. Like Gaston, who admires Belle solely for her beauty, the Bimbettes seem more focused on Gaston's appearance than on his behavior. They think Belle is crazy for not admiring him the way they do, and they continue to pursue him in spite of his determination to marry Belle.

The Enchantress

The Enchantress possesses incredible powers. She is able to transform both herself and others into different forms and can also see people's true feelings and desires. It was her reading of the Prince as a selfish young man that motivated her to visit him and ultimately curse his entire castle. But the Enchantress is not without sympathy and clearly believes in second chances. It is for this reason that she grants the Beast a way to break the curse: learning to love and being loved in return.

The Beast

Angry and rather violent, the Beast is at first glance just what his name implies: a beast. As a human prince, he was selfish and cold-hearted. It was these traits that brought on the Enchantress's curse. And his years of isolation in his palace have not helped soften him. If anything, his anger at his inability to break the curse and shame at his monstrous appearance have hardened him even more. The Beast is stubborn, gruff, quick to anger, and completely lacking in manners. But there is more hiding beneath the surface. In spite of his short temper, the Beast can actually be quite kind. He has been shown to have an incredibly gentle nature toward animals, including birds and horses, and he has a loving relationship with many of his servants. The more the Beast gets to know Belle, the more he wishes to make her feel welcome in his home. He gifts Belle his library simply because he knows it will make her happy, and he later allows her to leave the castle even though he knows it will likely result in his remaining a beast forever.

did you **know?**

- **The Beast's appearance draws inspiration from the mane of a lion, the head of a buffalo, the brow of a gorilla, the tusks of a wild boar, the legs and tail of a wolf, and the body of a bear.**

- **Some of the sculptures seen in the castle are early concept versions of the Beast.**

The Wardrobe

The Wardrobe resides in Belle's bedroom and often serves as a sounding board for Belle. She tries to convince Belle that the Beast is not as bad as he seems and is instrumental in getting Belle ready for her dinner with the Beast. The Wardrobe lives for fashion and has the clothes to prove it—her drawers contain something for every occasion, and jewels to match! Like the other enchanted objects, the Wardrobe dreams of breaking the curse and returning to her human form.

Chip

A little teacup with a chip in his rim, Chip is one of Belle's closest friends in the castle. The two love to explore together. Chip is quite young and has retained his childish curiosity about the world. He is full of questions and always ready for adventure. He also has an incredibly active imagination—so much so that his mother at first didn't believe him when he told her there was a girl in the castle. In spite of his age and size, Chip is very brave. He even goes so far as to stow away in Belle's bag when she leaves the castle, and it is he who rescues Belle and Maurice when they are locked up by an angry mob.

Mrs. Potts

Mrs. Potts is the castle's housekeeper. Along with Cogsworth, she keeps the castle running. Intelligent and level-headed, Mrs. Potts is perhaps the most reliable of the enchanted objects. She can always be counted on to do the right thing, regardless of any orders she may have received from the Beast. She is also the only member of the household who is willing to stand up to her master for his poor behavior. The Beast respects her for this and often changes his behavior as a result of her scolding. But it is not just the Beast she keeps in line. Mrs. Potts is not afraid to call out the other members of the castle staff—or her son, Chip—when they are doing something she doesn't approve of. Of all the enchanted objects, Mrs. Potts seems to understand the most about love. She takes Belle under her wing and carefully guides her toward liking, and eventually loving, the Beast.

did you **know?**

- **There are at least six enchanted teacups besides Chip, but it is not clear if they are all Mrs. Potts's children.**

- **Mrs. Potts makes a small cameo as a non-enchanted teapot at Jane Porter's camp in *Tarzan*. She also appears in *The Lion King 1½*, and there is a topiary shaped like her in *Meet the Robinsons*.**

- **Mrs. Potts's husband is never shown.**

Hiro Hamada

Fourteen-year-old Hiro Hamada is a robotics genius. He can build anything, although he doesn't always use his skills for good! In fact, Hiro has a tendency to use his bots to win money at illegal bot fights (although he'll be the first to tell you that the fights aren't illegal—only betting on them is!). Hiro can sometimes come across as brash and cocky. At other times he seems shy and socially awkward. Hiro has a hard time making friends. He also finds school to be boring and would rather teach himself, much to the chagrin of his Aunt Cass. This all changes when Hiro's older brother, Tadashi, introduces him to a world of new possibilities—and new friends—at the San Fransokyo Institute of Technology. When Tadashi dies tragically, Hiro finds himself the unwitting leader of a group of superheroes who come to be known as Big Hero 6.

did you **know?**

- **Hiro graduated from high school at thirteen years old.**

- **Baymax's scan of Hiro shows that he is slightly allergic to peanuts.**

- **Hiro's parents died when he was three.**

- **Hiro loves gummy bears.**

Tadashi Hamada

Kind, caring, and encouraging, Tadashi is the perfect role model for his brother, Hiro, a position he takes very seriously. But that doesn't stop his silly side from coming out on occasion. He is a gentle, understanding brother, but he is not above scolding Hiro when he does something wrong. Still, rather than just tell Hiro what's best for him, Tadashi prefers to find a way to get Hiro to realize it on his own. Tadashi is a student at the San Fransokyo Institute of Technology. Like Hiro, he is gifted at robotics. More than anything, he just wants to help people. To this end, he built and programmed a state-of-the-art health care companion robot, Baymax, who can diagnose and treat almost any ailment.

Aunt Cass

As owner of the popular Lucky Cat Café and full-time caregiver to two teenage boys, Aunt Cass is a bit overworked. But that doesn't stop her from always being ready with a laugh, a hug, or a home-cooked meal. Cass is upbeat and usually in a good mood, which she shows by being very talkative. She is also incredibly proud of Hiro and Tadashi, as she'll tell anyone who will listen. As loving as she is, Cass does tend to be a bit absentminded and can be oblivious to what is going on around her, as evidenced by Hiro's ability to sneak Baymax in and out of the house right under her nose.

Baymax

Baymax is a robotic health care companion. He was built by Tadashi Hamada to improve health care around the world. He is summoned by the sound of distress and can be dismissed with the words "I am satisfied with my care." Baymax will take his time thinking through even the simplest situations, and he has a tendency to get distracted by his curiosity about the world. Baymax's lack of understanding of human emotion or sarcasm means he tends to take things very literally. But it's the nurse chip, a special computer chip located where his heart would be, that really makes Baymax the lovable robot he is. This chip contains Baymax's memories and personality. Baymax cares deeply about Hiro and would do anything for him, as long as it doesn't go against his primary objective never to harm a human being.

did you **know?**

- **Without his armor, Baymax is six feet two inches tall.**
- **It took Tadashi eighty-four tries to perfect Baymax.**
- **Baymax makes a cameo in *Zootopia* as an antenna topper on Finnick's van. One of the Kakamora in *Moana* also has Baymax's face, as does a snowgie in *Frozen Fever*.**

Go Go Tomago

Go Go is a mechanical engineering student. She lives for speed and is willing to take on any challenge. Go Go is tough, athletic, and sarcastic. Her fierce attitude makes her somewhat unapproachable, and even her closest friends have a hard time getting her to open up. In spite of this, Go Go is a loyal and protective friend whose ability to think calmly and take control of a situation even when the odds are against her make her a natural leader. She also has a strong moral code and is willing to stand up to anyone who is doing what she deems unethical—even if that person is her friend.

Fred

This good-natured comic book enthusiast and monster movie fan is the son of a wealthy couple in San Fransokyo. Although his parents are often away, Fred has full access to the family mansion and fortune, which come in very handy for the members of Big Hero 6. Unlike his friends, Fred isn't a student at the San Fransokyo Institute of Technology—he's an English major at nearby SF State—but he does love science, and he puts his enthusiasm to good use as SFIT's mascot. His skill at twirling things is also surprisingly useful in combat.

Wasabi

Wasabi is a physics student at San Fransokyo Institute of Technology, where he channels his love for planning, precision, and organization into the science of creating lasers. Of all his friends, Wasabi appears to be the one with the most common sense. Wasabi is a neatnik who follows the rules and would prefer to take the time to think a situation out carefully rather than just jump in. He is also a bit jumpy and often gets scared in intense situations. But Wasabi is no coward. His fearfulness melts away in the face of danger posed to others, and he has shown on more than one occasion that he is willing to risk his own life for his friends. And while he'd always rather have a plan, he's pretty good at thinking on his feet and reacting quickly when necessary.

did you **know?**

- **Wasabi is six feet four inches tall.**
- **Wasabi got his nickname after he once spilled wasabi on his shirt.**
- **Wasabi is afraid of heights.**

Honey Lemon

Don't let Honey Lemon's funky glasses and eye-catching outfits fool you— there's a lot more to this Latina fashionista than her unique sense of style. A chemistry whiz with a can-do attitude and a love for explosive reactions, she's pretty much unstoppable! Honey is sweet, outgoing, and highly photogenic. She loves to take pictures of herself and her friends on her smartphone whenever she goes somewhere exciting. Honey is also an extreme optimist. She is the one who keeps her friends smiling, even when the going gets tough. Honey is the most observant of her friends and possesses excellent deductive skills. But her true passion is for chemistry— especially mixing up concoctions in the blink of an eye. This can give her a bit of a mad-scientist vibe, which she personally loves!

Mr. Yama

Mr. Yama is the undisputed champion of the bot fighting scene. He is sure that his bot, Little Yama, is the best in all of San Fransokyo, and he revels in rubbing his wins in his failed competitors' faces. His arrogance gets challenged, however, when he meets Hiro Hamada. Mr. Yama does not take well to losing, and he reveals his dangerous nature by siccing his goons on Hiro after the fight.

Robert Callaghan

A world-renowned scientist and professor at the San Fransokyo Institute of Technology, Robert Callaghan is a brilliant roboticist who serves as a mentor to Tadashi Hamada. Callaghan appears to be a kind, loving man determined to use science to change the world for the better, and this was once true. But when he loses his daughter in an accident allowed by Alistair Krei, everything changes. Bent on getting revenge on Krei, Callaghan's heart hardens and he eventually becomes the villain Yokai. As Yokai, the professor seemingly has no moral compass. He is coldhearted, completely lacking in compassion, and will stop at nothing to use his vast swarm of microbots to get the revenge he seeks—no matter whom he hurts. It is not until his final battle that he seems capable of even the smallest regret for the damage he has caused.

did you **know?**

- **According to a scan by Baymax, Robert Callaghan suffers from acute stress disorder and emotional instability. Baymax's scan also reveals that Callaghan has AB negative blood and weighs 173 pounds.**

- **The name Yokai is never spoken in the movie. Instead, he is referred to as "guy in the kabuki mask," "masked man," or "man in the mask."**

Abigail Callaghan

Abigail is the daughter of world-renowned scientist Robert Callaghan. As a child, she had a keen interest in bot fighting and technology, and when she grew up, she chose a career as a test pilot for Krei Tech. During a test flight for an experimental teleportation system, she was lost and presumed dead—an event that caused her father to spiral into grief and fury. But Abigail is not dead after all. Rather, she is suspended in a state of hyper sleep, from which she is awakened once rescued by Hiro and Baymax.

Alistair Krei

Entrepreneur, tech guru, and CEO of Krei Tech, Alistair Krei is always on the hunt for the next big thing. The charismatic Krei built his company from scratch, and he is very proud of it. But his business practices are somewhat questionable, and he's been accused of cutting corners and ignoring scientific evidence in order to save money. Krei is used to getting—or at least buying—his way, and does not like being told no. Even so, he isn't out to hurt anyone. He simply doesn't always consider the consequences of his actions.

Taran

Taran is an apprentice to the old farmer Dallben. He lives on a farm in the land of Prydain and looks after Hen Wen the pig. Taran dreams of becoming a brave warrior and proving himself through heroic deeds. When the Horned King steals Hen Wen, Taran sets off to rescue her. He manages to free Hen Wen but is captured himself. He meets Princess Eilonwy, who helps him escape, and he also finds a magical sword. Taran later gives the sword to the three witches, Orgoch, Orddu, and Orwne, in exchange for the Black Cauldron. With the help of Gurgi, Fflewddur Fflam, and Princess Eilonwy, Taran defeats the Horned King and destroys the power of the Black Cauldron. His taste for adventure satisfied, he heads home to Caer Dallben with his three new friends.

did you **know?**

- **Taran was a foundling discovered by Dallben.**

- **In the early development stages of the film, Taran's age varied between twelve, fifteen, and twenty. Finally, the animators settled on the age of fourteen.**

Fflewddur Fflam

Fflewddur Fflam is a minstrel whom Taran and Princess Eilonwy first meet in the Horned King's dungeons. He has a magic harp that breaks a string every time he tells a lie. After he is rescued by Taran and Eilonwy, he continues with them on their journey.

Gurgi

Gurgi is a small furry creature who loves apples, which he refers to as "munchings and crunchings." Gurgi is very cowardly and often runs away from a fight. But he eventually finds the courage to save his friends by sacrificing himself and jumping into the Black Cauldron—destroying both the Horned King and the Cauldron's powers. The witches revive Gurgi in exchange for the Black Cauldron.

The Horned King

The Horned King will stop at nothing to find the Black Cauldron so that he can raise an evil undead army of Cauldron-Born to destroy all living things in Prydain. He seeks to be a god among men. He also controls many evil forces, including the dragon-like Gwythaints, the green dwarf Creeper, and his henchmen. The Horned King has a ghoulish look with a skeletal body, two twisted horns on his head, and glowing red eyes. He wants to control Hen Wen so he can use her powers to locate the Black Cauldron. The Horned King's desire for power ultimately leads to his untimely demise, as he gets sucked into the Black Cauldron and destroyed.

did you **know?**

- **Although it is implied the Horned King is a sorcerer of some sort, he actually performs very little magic. He displays his powers only to teleport into his castle's mess hall and to call upon the spirit of the Black Cauldron.**

Princess Eilonwy

Princess Eilonwy has a magical orb that the Horned King thinks will lead him to the Black Cauldron. He captures her and throws her in the dungeons. Using her magic, she and Taran escape together. Eilonwy is chatty and strong-willed, which often causes her to clash with Taran. But she is also very compassionate and cares deeply for her friends. Over time, she comes to love Taran and is distraught when he offers to sacrifice himself to the Black Cauldron to save Prydain.

Hen Wen

This little pig has blue eyes and a big secret. She has magical powers and can see into the future. She lives with the old farmer Dallben and his apprentice, Taran. The Horned King wants to control her so that he can find the Black Cauldron. When she is captured by the Horned King, Taran sets off on a journey to rescue her from the villain's evil clutches.

Bolt

Having spent nearly his entire life isolated in a TV studio, Bolt is unaware of how to interact with other animals in the real world. He considers himself a very important individual, and as such, feels no need to take advice from others. This may be because to listen to anyone else would make him feel powerless, the opposite of the superhero he has always believed himself to be. When he is separated from his owner, Penny, Bolt is forced to let go of this persona, though, and accept that he is a normal dog in order to complete his mission of finding her. He must also learn to trust others and to behave like a loving, affectionate pet. Despite the way he changes, one fact remains the same: Bolt loves Penny. His dedication to her is unwavering, to the point of being willing to risk his own life for hers. This admirable quality makes him a dog anyone could love.

did you **know?**

- **In early versions of the film's story, Bolt was named Henry.**

- **The address on Bolt's tag is the real location of Disney's Feature Animation building.**

Mittens

Mittens was abandoned by her owners and left to fend for herself on the mean streets of New York City. She managed to survive by gaining control of several pigeons who bring her food in exchange for protection, but she was left with a strong distrust of humans. Sassy and short-tempered, Mittens cannot help being moved by Bolt's loyalty to Penny. It is she who teaches him how to be a real dog and ultimately helps Bolt find his way to Penny.

Rhino

This little hamster is Bolt's biggest fan. He has seen—and memorized—every episode of Bolt's show. So when the opportunity arises to help his hero, Rhino jumps at it. Rhino may not be the brightest creature, and tends to be a bit naive about the world, but he is eager to help and incredibly loyal. In fact, he helps both Bolt and Mittens out of several scrapes.

Penny

Thirteen-year-old Penny is a kind, lovable girl. She adopted Bolt when she was eight years old and the two have been inseparable ever since. The two are costars of the hit TV show *Bolt*. When Bolt runs away, mistakenly thinking Penny has been kidnapped, she is heartbroken. Penny is determined to find Bolt, much to the chagrin of her agent, who would rather she forget all about him and act against a look-alike dog. But Penny is as loyal to Bolt as he is to her. Luckily, true love wins out in the end, and the two are ultimately reunited.

did you **know?**

- **Penny is the name of the character she plays on *Bolt*. Her real name is not known.**

- **Miley Cyrus voices Penny in the final version of the film, but another actress was originally cast in the role and even recorded all the lines before Cyrus was brought on.**

King Fergus

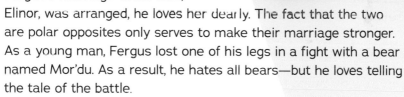

King Fergus is a loud, jolly man who gets along with most anyone. Although he often gets annoyed at the antics of his triplet sons, he knows how to have a good time and is actually quite patient. King Fergus loves fighting and is very happy to have raised a daughter who will stand up for herself. Although Fergus's marriage to his wife, Elinor, was arranged, he loves her dearly. The fact that the two are polar opposites only serves to make their marriage stronger. As a young man, Fergus lost one of his legs in a fight with a bear named Mor'du. As a result, he hates all bears—but he loves telling the tale of the battle.

Mor'du

Once an arrogant prince, Mor'du now lives his life as a monstrous bear. As a human, he allowed his pride to drive a rift between himself and his family. Unwilling to mend the bond he had broken, Mor'du found himself cursed to remain a bear forever. Although Mor'du is covered in black fur, his body features numerous scars—the result of his battles with humans, including King Fergus, over the years. He has one glowing yellow eye and one dead red eye. He has the strength of ten men and can only be stopped at last by another bear—Elinor, whose humanity shines through as she protects her daughter.

Merida

Headstrong and independent, Merida wants to do things her own way. Although she has a close relationship with her father and brothers, Merida's relationship with her mother is strained. She hates having to behave like a proper lady and finds the social etiquette her mother tries to teach her tedious. She also feels that her mother puts far too much emphasis on custom and what is expected of her as a princess, with no allowance for having fun. Merida would much rather spend her days in the woods, riding her horse, Angus, and practicing her archery. Despite her distaste for cultural customs, Merida is not totally willing to disregard the myths of her land. She finds the wisps intriguing and boldly follows them when they appear.

did you **know?**

- **Merida has more than 111,700 hairs on her head. If her hair were straightened, it would reach down past her knees.**

- **Throughout the movie, Merida wears a total of twenty-two different costumes and has five different hairstyles.**

Harris, Hubert, and Hamish

Merida's three younger brothers are always ready to stir up a little mischief. The identical triplets never speak, and only Merida and her mother can tell them apart. While Merida is expected to act like a lady, her brothers run around the castle causing trouble. The three love a good prank, from tying Fergus's wooden leg to the table to instigating a brawl between visiting lords. They are also particularly fond of sweets and can often be bribed to behave with the promise of dessert.

Angus

Black as night with a white muzzle and hooves, Angus is Merida's best friend and most trusted confidant. Like his mistress, Angus has a tendency to be stubborn. He has also shown himself at times to be easily scared. But Angus would never allow his fear to stop him from protecting Merida. He is fiercely loyal to her, as she is to him. The two share a strong, loving bond, so much so that Merida will not allow anyone else to see to his care.

Queen Elinor

Elinor is elegant and ladylike, as she believes a queen should be. She understands that her role in the kingdom is that of a diplomat and often steps in to resolve quarrels between her husband and neighboring lords. Her position requires her to be strict and stubborn—especially with Merida, whom she educates in the customs and traditions of their people. Elinor thinks that knowing her kingdom's history is important, as there is much to learn from the past, and she believes strongly that people should follow the path laid out for them rather than blazing their own way. She expects Merida to act like a princess and does not take kindly to Merida's insistence that she wants to do things differently. Like Merida, Elinor is strong-willed. However, she approaches challenges with the calmness befitting a queen rather than the rashness often shown by her daughter. It is not until she is turned into a bear, and later back into a human, that Elinor comes to accept the idea of Merida's following her own path.

did you **know?**

- **Elinor's name means "shining light" in Gaelic.**

- **The look of Elinor's dress was created by covering matted silk with metallic paint. This gave animation artists something to study when completing her gown.**

Lord and Wee Dingwall

T he scrappy, quick-tempered Lord Dingwall never lets his diminutive stature get in the way of solving problems. He wishes to be in charge at all times, loves a high-spirited fight, and has no problem taking on even the burliest adversary. Wee Dingwall, on the other hand, while loyal to his father, doesn't seem to have the same fighting spirit. He spends most of his time with his head in the clouds, unaware of what is going on around him. Any success he has—as in the archery competition, when he is vying for Merida's hand in marriage—seems entirely accidental.

Lord and Young MacGuffin

L ord MacGuffin is a man of few words, but those he does speak demand respect. He is considered the most reasonable and even-tempered of the kingdom's three lords. Lord MacGuffin likes to laugh, and little makes him laugh harder than a good brawl. His son, Young MacGuffin, is a calm, gentle lad. In spite of his great size and strength, he is incredibly shy and hates being the center of attention. Young MacGuffin speaks in a Scottish dialect that almost no one can understand and relies on his father to translate for him.

Lord and Young Macintosh

The Macintosh clan hails from the Scottish highlands. Lord Macintosh's body is covered in blue paint, and he usually wears a savage smile. A proud man, Lord Macintosh is quick to take offense at any perceived slight and is ready to jump into battle at any moment. Luckily, his bark is worse than his bite. His son, Young Macintosh, is incredibly sure of himself and his abilities, so much so that he often comes across as arrogant. He is also rather melodramatic and does not take well to losing. In spite of this, he is seemingly a kind man. He is incredibly loyal to his father and appears to value his friendships with Young MacGuffin and Wee Dingwall.

did you **know?**

- **The Macintosh clan's blue body paint follows a Pictish tradition. The paint is meant to give protection from swords in battle and provide strength against enemies.**

- **Young Macintosh is ambidextrous.**

Maudie

As nursemaid to Merida's three younger brothers, Maudie has her hands full. In addition to her duties caring for the children of the castle, she has also been seen to deliver messages to Queen Elinor. Maudie is easily frightened, and as a result has a hard time keeping the triplets in line. But she cares about the children and at times even serves as a sounding board for Merida.

The Witch

The Witch is a wood-carver by trade. She lives in a small hut in the woods with her pet crow and relies on her knowledge of magic to help with her work. Although she dislikes being asked to do magic for others, she is willing to perform her spells for a fee. The Witch is neither good nor bad. She simply gives her customers what they want—although not always in the way they may expect.

Dot

Princess Dot is the younger daughter of the Queen of Ant Island. Although her position as princess affords her some respect within the community, she has no actual authority. Dot is much younger than her sister, Atta, and as such, her wings are not yet fully developed. Her inability to fly is a constant source of frustration for her. But Dot is persistent. No matter how many times she falls down, she continues to get up. She won't let her failure stop her from trying again to make her wings work. Dot idolizes the local inventor, Flik, and believes in his inventions even when no one else does.

did you **know?**

- **One of the creators of *A Bug's Life* said he wanted a little girl in the film because he had just had a daughter.**

- **An image of Dot can be seen in Al's abstract painting in *Toy Story 2*.**

Atta

Atta is the elder daughter of the Queen and heir to the throne of Ant Island. She takes this role seriously and worries endlessly about doing a good job. Atta is obsessed with perfection. She thinks the only way to make her subjects like her is never to make a mistake. She is particularly concerned about the food offering to the grasshoppers and quickly grows frustrated with Flik's accidental interference. But no one can be stressed all the time, and even the nervous Atta eventually learns to unwind, thanks to some advice from her mother and a blooming relationship with Flik.

The Queen

The Queen is a kind, caring ruler with a good sense of humor. She loves her daughters dearly and is equally fond of her pet aphid, Aphie. While Atta frets about ruling wisely and focuses on every little detail, the Queen takes a much more laid-back approach. She has been ruling Ant Island long enough to know that not everything always goes to plan. Her years of experience have taught her how to joke about bad situations—as long as she is able to get the situation under control. But the Queen is not entirely without concern. She fears that Dot will hurt herself by trying to fly too soon and worries about Atta settling into her new role as Queen. Still, the Queen is happy to hand her crown over to Atta when the time is right.

Flik

More than anything, Flik just wants to make a difference to the ant colony's way of life—to make life *easier*. A nerdy, inventive guy with a can-do attitude, Flik focuses his energies on a whole host of inventions meant to help the colony. Unfortunately, his inventions tend to go awry, leaving situations worse off than they started. This bothers Flik greatly, as he is desperate to impress Princess Atta, who seemingly wants nothing to do with him. Flik counts among his friends Princess Dot and the circus bugs he brings back to the colony to fight the grasshoppers. He is a loyal bug who would do anything for his friends. Flik proves this when he stands up against the grasshopper Hopper to save Dot, and again when he bravely leads Hopper to his doom.

did you **know?**

- **Flik makes an appearance in the blooper reel during the credits of *Toy Story 2*. A car version of Flik also appears in the epilogue of *Cars*.**

- **In the first draft of *A Bug's Life*, Flik was a red ant named Red who was part of the circus troupe.**

Manny

Manny is a praying mantis with an English accent. He also happens to be a magician and a member of P. T. Flea's traveling circus troupe. Manny's act involves the "Chinese Cabinet of Metamorphosis," which is really the packaging from Chinese takeout. He takes his work very seriously and does not appreciate being mocked or doubted. Manny also possesses impressive acting skills, as he shows when he pretends to die during a bird attack. Manny is generally kind and courteous to everyone. The one exception is Flik, whom he takes an immediate dislike to. His opinion changes over time, however, and he agrees to help rid the ant colony of the grasshoppers once and for all.

Gypsy

A slender, beautiful moth, Gypsy is married to Manny and works as his assistant in their magic show. Gypsy is exceedingly kind and has no taste for gore or violence. In spite of this, she is incredibly brave and would do anything for her fellow circus bugs. Gypsy's wings have the power to stun and distract people, an ability she uses to her advantage on more than one occasion.

Dim

A rhinoceros beetle, Dim serves as the transportation for several of the other circus performers, including Heimlich, Rosie, and Tuck and Roll. Dim has a childish nature and is easily upset. He sobs in pain when he is injured and happily lets Rosie pamper him. He is also incredibly ticklish, especially on his thorax. Although Dim's primary role in the circus is to get the performers from place to place, he also stars in an act with Rosie.

did you **know?**

- **Dim's horn structure wasn't meant to be reflective of a specific kind of horned beetle. However, in 2006, entomologist Brett C. Ratcliffe discovered a species of rhinoceros beetle, *Megaceras briansaltini*, that closely resembles Dim. Ratcliffe called this instance of nature imitating art "the Dim effect."**

- **A toy of Dim can be seen in the toy store in *Toy Story 2*.**

P. T. Flea

P. T. Flea is the ringmaster of the circus. Although just a little flea, he considers himself far more important than any of the other performers. Mr. Flea loves money and has a hard time parting with it. As a result, he has a long-standing policy: he won't give refunds if a show lasts more than two minutes. Mr. Flea's grand finale is an act called Flaming Death. The first time he performed it was an accident, and he nearly burned to death. But his audience loved it, so he added it as a permanent staple of the show. After all, he's willing to do anything as long as he's paid for it!

Tuck and Roll

A pair of Hungarian pill bugs, Tuck and Roll neither speak nor understand English. In fact, the language they *do* speak seems to be primarily gibberish. Although the two occasionally argue, they are usually the best of friends. They act as cannonballs in P. T. Flea's Flaming Death act. Unfortunately, their arguing causes the entire act to go off the rails, nearly killing Mr. Flea. The only way to tell these twins apart is by their eyebrows. Tuck has two eyebrows, while Roll has a unibrow.

Rosie

R osie is a black widow spider. Her primary role in the circus is as part of an act in which she performs as a rhinoceros trainer. Her partner in this act is Dim. Outside of performing, Rosie tends to be the mother figure of the group. She happily comforts Dim when he is upset and does the same for several of the younger ants in the colony. Rosie dislikes conflict and finds herself particularly annoyed with Tuck and Roll's arguments. She has been married twelve times. Each of her husbands has died, making her, as she says, "a black widow widow."

Francis

F rancis performs as a clown in the circus. This ladybug has a short temper. His biggest pet peeve is the fact that other bugs are always mistaking him for a girl, and he has even been known to pick fights with audience members over their confusion. But Francis has a softer side. He saves Dot from a bird and is later elected honorary den mother for the Blueberries, a role he grudgingly accepts and even comes to enjoy. Francis is close friends with Slim and Heimlich, both of whom help him keep his anger in check. He carries Slim when the circus troupe flies.

Heimlich

Heimlich is a fat green caterpillar with an enormous appetite. He works as a clown and hates performing on an empty stomach. He has even been known to ask audience members if he can finish their food. In spite of the fact that Heimlich is easily frightened, he shows great bravery in standing up to the grasshoppers. His dream is to become a beautiful butterfly, and he does in fact ultimately sprout wings. Unfortunately, his extreme weight makes it impossible for him to fly.

did you **know?**

- **Heimlich makes an appearance in _Toy Story 2_. He can be seen crawling along a branch just before Buzz Lightyear chops it down.**

Slim

A cinnamon brown stick insect, Slim is used as a prop in the circus rather than having an act of his own. Slim is a nervous guy. As a result, he is often reprimanded by P. T. Flea. He is best friends with Heimlich and Francis, and relies on Francis to help him get from place to place when the circus moves. That is because, unlike most stick insects, Slim does not have wings and therefore cannot fly. In spite of his nerves, Slim is a nice bug. He treats others with respect and often finds himself stepping in to break up fights started by Francis.

Molt

Molt is Hopper's younger brother. He got his name due to the fact that his chitin exoskeleton molts off in flakes. According to Molt, he is vice president of the grasshopper gang. Unfortunately, he's the only one who seems to believe that! Molt tries hard to be scary, but no one takes him seriously. In fact, he is actually quite good-hearted. His kind nature regularly infuriates Hopper, who reminds him that the only reason he is still alive is because Hopper promised their mother on her deathbed that he wouldn't kill Molt. This loud-mouthed, gullible grasshopper ultimately sees the light and finds the place he truly belongs: the circus!

Hopper

The leader of the grasshoppers, Hopper is ruthless and violent. He thinks nothing of killing ants, whom he considers to be beneath him and good only for gathering food. Hopper dislikes being thought of as weak in any way and is not above hurting his own men to make himself look stronger. But Hopper is not just brawn. He's got brains, too. Hopper works hard to keep the ants fearing him because he knows that, in reality, they outnumber his grasshoppers. If they ever decided to turn on him, Hopper knows he wouldn't stand a chance.

did you **know?**

- **Hopper's right eye was damaged in an incident where he was nearly eaten by a bird.**

- **Hopper is among Pixar's most ruthless villains. He was also the first Pixar character to die.**

Lightning McQueen

With seven Piston Cup wins and a passion for motorsports, Lightning McQueen has earned the reputation of a world champion. Lightning used to think that winning was everything. He was arrogant and obnoxious, with no regard for anyone else's feelings. But his time in Radiator Springs has taught him what's really important, like true friends. Lightning values time with his girlfriend, Sally, and his friends in Radiator Springs. He learned most of what he knows about racing from the late great Doc Hudson, and he is looking forward to passing this knowledge on as he enters the next phase of his career.

did you **know?**

- **Lightning's racing number was originally going to be 57, as a reference to John Lasseter's birth year, but the filmmakers decided to change it to 95.**

- **Lightning is named after deceased Pixar supervising animator Glenn McQueen.**

- **Lightning originally did not think he needed headlights, because racers always race in lit stadiums.**

Mack

If there is one vehicle that has been with Lightning McQueen since nearly the very beginning, it's Mack. Although he's technically a race transporter, Mack is so much more than just a part of Team McQueen. Mack is McQueen's confidant, his good friend, and his sounding board. He's always reliable, always there, and always ready to roll, whether it's getting McQueen to the Piston Cup championship or transporting him all the way to the Florida 500.

Mater

Mater is a good ol' car with a big heart. He runs Tow Mater Towing and Salvage and manages the local impound lot. Though a little rusty, he has the quickest tow rope in Carburetor County and is always the first to lend a helping hook. Mater doesn't have a mean bolt on his chassis. He sees the bright side of any situation; Radiator Springs just wouldn't be the same without him. Although Mater sometimes seems a bit dim-witted, he knows everything there is to know about cars, engines, and towing, and often finds himself offering surprisingly wise advice to his friends. Mater's not only Lightning McQueen's best friend but also his biggest fan. Even when Lightning is on the road, Mater is always only a phone call away—that is, when he isn't in the pit helping out his buddy.

Luigi

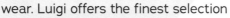

Luigi runs Luigi's Casa Della Tires, the local tire shop in Radiator Springs. If you're going to drive through this world, why not look good doing it? That's Luigi's motto. Cars may not get to choose their make and model, but they all have a choice when it comes to the tires they wear. Luigi offers the finest selection west of the Mississippi. Luigi's Casa Della Tires is known far and wide for impeccable service, a wide range of whitewalls, and of course its very stylish owner. He now travels with Guido and Lightning McQueen during the racing season and helps Lightning with all his tire needs.

Guido

Besides being part of Luigi's Casa Della Tires, Guido dreamed of being part of a pit crew for a real race car—a dream that came true when he became part of Lightning McQueen's crew. He and Luigi were there every mile of the journey to help Lightning prepare for the Florida 500. One of these days, Guido hopes to set a new world record for the fastest pit stop turnaround of all time.

Doc Hudson

D oc Hudson, the Fabulous Hudson Hornet, was a car of few words but many talents. With his crew chief and sponsor, Smokey, Hud (his nickname during his legendary racing days) won three Piston Cups and held the record for most wins in a single season. Later, he not only served as Radiator Springs' judge but also as the resident doctor. Doc was respected and admired by the townsfolk for the way he looked after them. It wasn't until a hotshot rookie racer named Lightning McQueen roared into town that the other side of the ol' judge was revealed. Despite a rocky start, Doc and Lightning became great friends and an unstoppable racing team.

did you **know?**

- **His license plate is 51HHMD, which is a reference to his year and track number (51), model (Hudson Hornet) and profession (medical doctor).**

- **Doc started racing in the Piston Cup series in 1951.**

- **A blue Hudson Hornet can be seen in *The Incredibles*. Even though *Cars* was released after *The Incredibles*, development of the film was already well under way.**

Fillmore

Fillmore is Radiator Springs' resident hippie. A believer in individuality and all things natural, he brews his own organic fuel and preaches about its many benefits. Visitors can try Fillmore's special flavors in the tasting room behind his love-bead and tie-dye-covered geodesic dome. His many conspiracy theories and "naturally" unkempt yard drive his neighbor Sarge absolutely crazy.

Sarge

Sarge loves to tell stories about his daring fearlessness in the military. One time, a tank friend of his lost a belt in the Battle of the Bulge, and Sarge towed him to safety. For his bravery, Sarge received the Grille Badge of True Metal! This and medals like it are displayed front and center at Sarge's Surplus Hut, right next to Sarge's very own Mother Road Survival Kit. He guarantees that if you break down, his kit will get you through the night—or the next world war. Even better, it all stows nicely in your trunk.

Flo

Flo first arrived in Radiator Springs as a touring Motorama girl in the 1950s. She was headed west with a group of models when her chaperone had fuel-pump problems just outside of town. Flo and the other show-car girls spent an unforgettable night in Radiator Springs. While she was there, Flo's paint got scratched. But when she went to Ramone for a paint job, he refused to give her one. It wasn't because he was too good to paint her but because she was too good to be painted. When the girls left, Flo stayed. She and Ramone have been together ever since. Flo runs Flo's V-8 Café, the only traditional gas station for miles around.

Ramone

A true artist isn't afraid to take chances, to explore new ways to express himself, or to push the limits of culture. Ramone believes that the automotive body can be a vehicle of expression. Every day gives him an opportunity to explore new paint jobs and to push the limitless boundaries of his art. Ramone is the proud owner of Ramone's House of Body Art, located right across the street from Flo's V-8 Café.

Sally

Sally is the heart and soul of Radiator Springs. She used to be a high-powered attorney in Los Angeles but grew tired of her hectic life and decided to find something more peaceful. These days, Sally serves as the local attorney. She also owns and runs the Cozy Cone Motel and Wheel Wagon Motel. In spite of her busy schedule, she still finds time to check in on everybody in Radiator Springs and see her boyfriend, Lightning McQueen.

did you **know?**

• **Sally is a 2002 Porsche 911 Carrera. Her top speed is 177 miles per hour.**

• **Sally was originally going to be a Mustang. She was later changed to a Porsche, since the grille looked more feminine.**

Lizzie

When Lizzie rolled into Radiator Springs, it was love at first sight—love for the town itself and for Stanley, the town's founder. But she kept Stanley on the soft shoulder for months. Then one day, Lizzie realized that Stanley's vision for a new oasis in the desert had become her dream, too. From that day on, they became the heart and soul of the town— and a couple who were never apart. Lizzie runs the local curio shop. She is a kind, grandmotherly woman who loves to talk, although she often has a hard time remembering things.

Red

Red may not be a fire truck of many words, but what he doesn't say he shows through his generous actions. Whether it's putting out a tire fire or caring for the beautiful flowers of Radiator Springs, Red is there to support and protect his beloved town. Red takes negative comments about his town very personally. So if you have something bad to say about Radiator Springs, you'd better watch out. Because if there's one thing Red is not afraid of, it's his emotions.

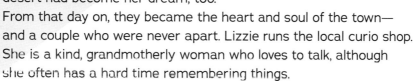

Sheriff

There's a long history of law enforcement in Sheriff's family. His father was a traffic cop and so were his aunt, his uncle, his two cousins on his mother's side, and his little brother. Even his grandfather was a traffic cop, in New York around the turn of the century. Sheriff is a no-nonsense, by-the-book type of car. He can't stand lawbreakers and will happily ticket those who don't abide by the laws of Radiator Springs.

Bessie

Bessie is Radiator Springs' resident road-paving machine. Everyone agrees she's a low-maintenance gal, but more than one unsuspecting hitcher has learned her quirks the hard way. Doc likes to say laying asphalt with Bessie is more like dancing than paving. Fill her with kerosene, gravel, and tar, and she'll produce the most beautiful ribbon of blacktop you've ever laid rubber on. But you don't want to pull her too fast or get her steamed up. Bessie carries two huge buckets of molten tar and she knows how to use them. Just ask Lightning McQueen!

Chick Hicks

C hick Hicks is a racing veteran with a chip on his shoulder. He cheated his way into more second-place finishes than any other car. Rude and arrogant, he was always sure he was the best racer out there, and was willing to go to any length to prove it. No trick was too underhanded for Chick. These days, Chick has retired from Piston Cup racing and signed on to the Racing Sports Network to host his own show. Instead of cutting down opponents on the track, he cuts them down verbally on his cable-run sports show, *Chick's Picks with Chick Hicks*. If you want the no-holds-barred commentary, Chick is your car!

Strip "The King" Weathers

F rom his humble beginnings on the Piston Cup circuit to the glitzy sponsorship and media attention, Strip Weathers (also known as The King) has seen it all. This racing champion won seven Piston Cups. Unlike his competitors, he raced honestly. Cheating never would have occurred to him. His career ended in a crash at a Piston Cup Championship and, truth be told, The King is enjoying his retirement. He loves spending more time with his queen, Mrs. The King.

Dusty Rust-Eze

Dusty and his brother, Rusty, are the owners of Rust-eze Medicated Bumper Ointment and the proud ten-year sponsors of racing superstar Lightning McQueen. They have believed in the racer ever since he was a rookie phenomenon. When the Next-Gen racers come along, Dusty and Rusty stick by McQueen's side and encourage him to keep following his dreams.

Rusty Rust-Eze

Rusty and his brother, Dusty, are the kings of Rust-eze. And they will do whatever it takes to make sure that Lightning McQueen has the tools he needs to be successful on the racetrack . . . even if it means releasing Lightning so he can pursue his dreams.

Francesco Bernoulli

Francesco grew up in the shadow of the famous Monza racecourse in Italy, where he and his friends would sneak onto the track and race the famous Pista di Alta Velocita bank turn. He was an instant winner on the amateur circuit and soon became an international Formula racer champion. The ladies love Francesco's open wheels, youngsters admire his winning spirit, and fellow racers envy his speed. But Francesco's biggest fan is Francesco himself, as evidenced by his racing number.

did you **know?**

- **Francesco's top speed is 220 miles per hour.**

- **On Francesco's side is a logo presenting the letters FR in a design similar to the F1 logo. It is the abbreviation of "Formula Racer," his racing league.**

- **Francesco prefers to speak about himself in third person. He is just that important!**

Carla Veloso

C arla hails from Rio de Janeiro, Brazil. The sweet but powerful Latin diva can dance the night away at "Car-nival," but she spends most of her time on the racetrack. After setting a new track record at the local Interlagos circuit, she was drafted to join the twenty-four-hour endurance racing team in Europe, where she posted a consistent series of podium finishes. Carla is one of the few female racers and is out to prove that she can keep up with the guys.

Shu Todoroki

S hu Todoroki is a Le Motor Prototype racer. He was raised at the base of the active Mount Asama volcano in Japan and soon became a champion on the Suzuka circuit. His sleek design sports a fiery red Ka-Riu dragon, which Shu borrowed from Japanese legend because he relates to its quiet yet fierce nature. His team legacy is filled with victories; his coach was the only Japanese car to ever win at Le Mans.

Raoul ÇaRoule

K nown as the "World's Greatest Rally Car," #6 Raoul ÇaRoule was born in Alsace, France. A restless soul, Raoul joined the famous Cirque du Voiture French circus where he studied *gymkhana*—a graceful, drift-filled motor sport that taught him pinpoint timing and an unparalleled ability to navigate tricky courses with ease. He was the first car to ever win nine consecutive rallies.

Jeff Gorvette

J eff Gorvette is one of the greatest race cars alive. His ability to succeed on the big ovals as well as on the road courses has made him respected around the world. Having moved from his hometown of Vallejo, California, to Indiana to be closer to the racing world, Gorvette's ability to succeed at all levels at such a young age has turned hoods wherever he competes. His "Rookie of the Year" awards and number of top ten finishes are unmatched.

Nigel Gearsley

Nigel Gearsley, from Warwickshire, England, is an Aston Martin DBR9 racer bearing #9. He got his start racing the Speed Hill Climb—a unique, completely uphill race that his family has run for generations through the Aston Hill mountain area. Nigel's racing career has been anything but an uphill challenge, as he's won nearly every start in the past few years on the Grand Touring Sports Car circuit, including a string of podiums at Nürburgring and Le Mans.

Max Schnell

Max Schnell started as a humble production sedan from Stuttgart. An avid amateur racer, Max would practice alone on the back roads of the dense Black Forest—a trek that one day caught the eye of a racing team owner. Soon Max was on a professional circuit, and as his horsepower increased, he converted himself to carbon fiber, dropping his weight and getting into prime racing shape. He's won more races at Motorheimring than any other World Touring Champion League car in history. A naturally brilliant engineer, he used logic and analytics to refine his build, making him a perfectly calibrated race car.

Miguel Camino

Spain's most famous, admired, and lusted over car is Pamplona's Miguel Camino. The GT2 caught the eye of the entire country while participating in the Running of the Bulldozers. Initially, he was just a fan, but he soon found himself in the ring with the dozers. His flair, style, and speed as a toreador inspired a generation of young bulldozer fighters, and soon, that same speed and flair turned heads on the racing circuit. Open and funny, Miguel is the life of any party.

Lewis Hamilton

Lewis Hamilton, the famously sleek and seriously fast #2 Grand Touring Sports champion, has been a determined and winning racer for most of his young life. Lewis spent his childhood going to school, taking karate lessons, and winning the British Karting championship by the age of ten. He continues to bring an exceptional work ethic and soft-spoken confidence to the racecourse, where his extraordinary achievements speak for themselves via a spotless track record on the junior and professional circuits. He carries the flag of Grenada, home to his family, who immigrated to Britain in the 1950s. His unrivaled technical skills, natural speed, and cool karate-inspired attitude make him a powerful contender.

Uncle Topolino

In the small village of Santa Ruotina near Porto Corsa, Italy, Luigi's favorite uncle, Topolino, lives with his beloved wife, Mama Topolino. Uncle Topolino is the owner of the village's tire shop. He taught Luigi and Guido everything they know, though Uncle Topolino is full of sage advice about more than just tires.

Mama Topolino

To all who know her, Luigi's aunt, Mama Topolino, is a masterful cook with the best fuel in the village of Santa Ruotina. She has a loving but fiery relationship with her husband, Uncle Topolino, and she shows her love and generosity for both family and friends by feeding everyone her renowned *delizioso* fuel.

Cruz Ramirez

Cruz Ramirez is a top-notch trainer at the Rust-eze Racing Center, where she's assigned to train the team's talented rookies. Her unconventional training methods have helped many young Piston Cup racers meet their goals on the track. Cruz once had racing dreams of her own, but it isn't until she meets Lightning McQueen that she realizes her passion to compete is still there. Now she'll finally get the chance to see if she's got what it takes to win.

did you **know?**

- **Cruz's nickname is the Maestro of Motivation.**

Chase Racelott

Next-generation Piston Cup racer Chase Racelott knows what it takes to win and was racing long before he ever set tire on a professional speedway. Like his fellow rookies, Chase knows how to push toward the front by combining his skills, track smarts, and top-of-the-line technology.

Jackson Storm

Cocky and sure of himself, Jackson Storm is a young Piston Cup rookie with his eyes focused solely on the championship. Coming out of nowhere in the racing world, Storm trained primarily on high-tech simulators. He displays refined technique but little practical wisdom on the track. Winning has come all too easy to Storm, so he's unable to fathom defeat—yet. His overconfidence may be his ultimate downfall.

did you **know?**

- **Jackson Storm won ten races in a row before winning his first Piston Cup.**

- **Jackson beat a racing record when he reached 213 miles per hour in a practice lap!**

Danny Swervez

Danny Swervez is a young racer who rose up against all odds to quickly climb the Piston Cup ladder. He is focused, eager to learn, and set on pushing himself to overcome obstacles both on and off the track. Danny is new to the racing scene but is a quick learner who strives to be the very best. He came in halfway through the racing season to take the place of Bobby Swift.

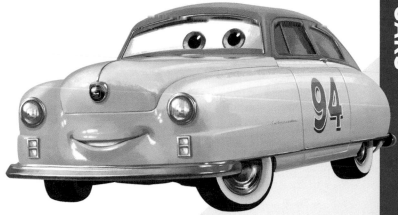

Louise "Barnstormer" Nash

Louise "Barnstormer" Nash was known as the First Lady of Racing in the early days of the Piston Cup. She won three races in a row in her first season against Doc Hudson. As one of the first and only females in racing at the time, it wasn't an easy road for Louise. She had to steal her racing number to get her first chance on the track. But Louise's fearless driving style soon won her the respect of every car she raced. Sassy and fun-loving, she still enjoys kicking off her hubcaps and racing at top speed.

Junior "Midnight" Moon

Long before official stock car tracks existed, souped-up jalopies raced for fun on wooded back roads with only the moon to light their way. That's where Junior Moon got his start and his name. Junior raced by his own rules. Hud and all the other early Piston Cup competitors truly loved to race with him.

Smokey

Smokey is a Piston Cup team owner, a crew chief, and the best dang mechanic in town. He also helped put Thomasville and a rookie racer known as the Fabulous Hudson Hornet on the map back in the 1950s. Smokey is known for his crafty tactics at the track, and the tales about his racing ingenuity seem to grow a bit taller with each telling. He has a gruff exterior and a very strong opinion when it comes to what he feels is right or wrong, but he often wrestles between going with his head (logic) and his gut (instinct), sometimes leaving his heart out by mistake. One thing is for sure: Smokey always wants to do right by his friends.

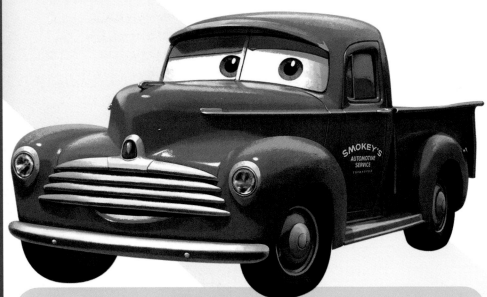

did you **know?**

- **Smokey's garage has been called "the Best Dang Garage in Town."**

River Scott

River Scott came from modest beginnings, but he always made the very best of what he had. With seven circuit wins from the early 1950s, his unique body style made him a trailblazer in the Piston Cup. He was scrappy and improvisational, and wore his dents proudly as symbols of what he had been through. He was Doc's racing contemporary and friend, and loves to tell tales of the good old days.

Sterling

Sterling is a smart and dashing business car who runs one of the largest racing centers in the country. Despite his wealth and influence, he comes across as unassuming and laid-back. Sterling often waves off formalities, choosing to be called Sterling over sir or mister. Although he's not cutthroat or power-hungry, his decisions will always be driven by what is best for his business. Sterling has invested a lot of money in Lightning McQueen, and he wants to make sure his investment pays off.

Chicken Little

Chicken Little is a bit of an outcast. After an incident with a hexagon-shaped object falling from the sky and an all-out panic that the sky was falling, he became the laughingstock of the town and the target of bullies. Chicken Little is eager to change his image, even going so far as to join the baseball team to make amends with his father and become popular, but he can't change his true nature. He worries about everything and can't help calling everyone else's attention to the things he is concerned about.

did you **know?**

- **His full name is Ace "Chicken Little" Cluck.**

- **In the original script, Chicken Little was written as a girl. This was changed to introduce a father–son dynamic to the film.**

Foxy Loxy

Foxy is the class monitor and a star baseball player. As far as she is concerned, there are only three things in the world that matter: being popular, being famous, and having good hair. Although she bullies Chicken Little and seems to take great joy in tormenting people, she does appear to have a softer side and has been known on occasion to show kindness to others. Foxy Loxy's best friend is Goosey Loosey, and Foxy appears to become the girlfriend of Runt of the Litter.

Goosey Loosey

Goosey Loosey is a white goose with a long neck. She is usually seen wearing a red dress with red hair bows. She also never speaks. Instead, Goosey quacks, honks, and squawks. Goosey's best friend is Foxy Loxy. Together, the two enjoy playing baseball and bullying and teasing the weaker kids, especially Chicken Little.

Abby Mallard

Abby is a duck. She has buck teeth, an asymmetrical face, and a slight speech impediment. As a result, the mean kids at school call her the Ugly Duckling. Abby is used to being teased and does her best to ignore it. She prefers to take an optimistic approach to life. Abby is Chicken Little's best friend. She stands by him no matter what and does her best to help him mend his relationship with his father. She also secretly has a crush on him.

Runt of the Litter

Runt of the Litter, a nine-hundred-pound pig, is one of Chicken Little's best friends. Kind and loyal, he stands by his friend no matter what. Runt is much bigger than the other children but far smaller than the rest of his family. He is easily frightened and prone to panic attacks. In spite of Foxy Loxy's bullying, Runt has a crush on her and ultimately succeeds in winning her over.

Fish Out of Water

Fish Out of Water is a goldfish who lives on land. He wears a scuba helmet filled with water. Fish is unable to speak. Instead, he makes gurgling sounds and acts out his feelings. In spite of his size, Fish is incredibly brave and outgoing.

Buck Cluck

Buck "Ace" Cluck is Chicken Little's father. He is a heavyset rooster who can usually be seen sporting a plaid dress shirt, black tie, and large brown pants. Buck's wife died when Chicken Little was young, and Buck never really learned to relate to his son. Buck would like Chicken Little to forget all the nonsense about the sky falling and throw himself into something worthwhile, like baseball.

Cinderella

Cinderella's mother died when she was just a young girl. Her father, believing his daughter needed a mother, married Lady Tremaine and brought her and her daughters to live with the family. But when Cinderella's father died, too, Lady Tremaine took over the household, making Cinderella no more than a serving girl in her own home. Cinderella's only friends are her dog, Bruno, and the mice and birds that live in her attic room. She enjoys sewing little outfits for the mice and always makes sure to save them some food. In spite of the harsh treatment she receives from her stepfamily, Cinderella remains a kind, loving girl. She makes the most of her situation and remains hopeful that she will one day find love and be whisked away from her evil stepfamily. Her life is turned upside down in the best way possible when an invitation comes from the King for all eligible maidens to attend a ball at the palace.

did you **know?**

- **Long before the feature film, there were plans to produce a Silly Symphony cartoon based on the story of Cinderella.**

- **The transformation of Cinderella's torn dress into a beautiful gown fit for a princess is said to be Walt Disney's favorite piece of animation ever.**

Anastasia

Slender with fair skin and red hair, Anastasia is known for always wearing shades of pink and magenta. She is Cinderella's stepsister and seems to take great joy in tormenting her. Anastasia has grown up pampered by her mother. As a result, she is lazy, selfish, and spoiled. She has grown accustomed to having Cinderella do everything for her. But Anastasia is not all bad. She has a romantic side and dreams of finding someone who will love her for who she really is.

Drizella

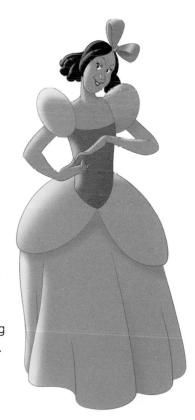

Drizella is tall and skinny, with dark brown hair. She is known for wearing shades of yellow, blue, and green. Unlike her sister, who does have a soft side, Drizella is ugly inside and out. She is jealous of Cinderella's beauty and would happily do anything to ruin her stepsister's life. Drizella is incredibly vain. She is sure she is one of the most beautiful maidens in the land and that the Prince will fall in love with her. Drizella learned about what's important from her mother. As far as she's concerned, the only thing that matters is marrying well and improving her social standing.

Lady Tremaine

Lady Tremaine is the epitome of grace and self-control. She believes that a lady must keep her composure at all times, as she frequently reminds her daughters. Lady Tremaine's chief goal in life is to see her daughters married well. She envies Cinderella's charm and beauty, and sees the girl as competition for her daughters. As far as she's concerned, the best way to remove the competition is to remove Cinderella from the social class in which she and her daughters travel. As a servant, Cinderella would not be of any interest to the men who might woo Anastasia and Drizella. Although she never physically hurts Cinderella, Lady Tremaine knows how to manipulate a situation to inflict the maximum amount of emotional pain. She expects absolute obedience from all three of her daughters and grows infuriated when any of them disobey her.

did you **know?**

- **Lady Tremaine makes a cameo on one of the menus in the *Who Framed Roger Rabbit* Special Edition DVD, but does not appear in the film itself.**

- **Lady Tremaine's name is mentioned only once throughout the course of *Cinderella*, when the young ladies and their parents are announced at the ball.**

Lucifer

Lucifer is Lady Tremaine's extremely spoiled cat. His only loyalty is to his mistress, who pampers him and treats him like royalty. Lucifer takes after Lady Tremaine and seems to have an extreme dislike for Cinderella. He tries to get her into trouble and often seems to go out of his way to make her life more difficult. But he has also shown dislike for Lady Tremaine's daughters. Lucifer is clever and cunning. His greatest joy in life is to track down and try to eat the mice that Cinderella takes care of.

Bruno

Cinderella has had Bruno ever since she was a young girl. The two grew up together under the cruel hand of Lady Tremaine. Bruno is very loyal to Cinderella. He dislikes Anastasia and Drizella for the way they treat her and has little patience for Lucifer. This seems to go both ways, as Lucifer is always coming up with plans to get Bruno in trouble and have him kicked out of the house.

The Fairy Godmother

Cinderella's fairy godmother is a kind, motherly woman with a pure heart and an optimistic outlook on life. Though wise in her own way, she has a tendency to forget important details—like where she put her wand and what her magic words are—and overlook things that would be obvious to anyone else. But once she remembers what she's doing, the Fairy Godmother is quick to act. She is also capable of incredible magic, even if it does have a time limit. The Fairy Godmother believes in helping those in need. She does not look kindly on people—or animals—who are cruel to others.

did you **know?**

- **The Fairy Godmother's design underwent so many changes that no one is sure what her original incarnation looked like.**

- **The Fairy Godmother presided over the official coronation and welcoming to the Disney Princess franchise of both Tiana and Rapunzel.**

The King

The King has a passionate temper. He has been known to be fairly unreasonable in his requests, and grows quite angry when things do not go his way. But he is also a romantic and a believer in love at first sight. The King had a very close relationship with his son when the Prince was young, but they grew apart as the Prince grew older. More than anything, he wants his son to marry and have children. Although this desire is in part due to a wish to see his son happy, the King will readily admit that he misses the sound of children running through the halls of the palace and he wants dearly to be a grandfather.

The Grand Duke

The Grand Duke is a dignified, intelligent subject to the King. He bases his opinions largely on reason and logic, in direct contrast to the King's emotionally driven decision-making. Although he doesn't always agree with the services the King asks him to perform, the Grand Duke is loyal to the King and does as he's told—possibly because he fears the King's wrath. However, he does seem to genuinely care about the King, as he tries to act as a voice of reason and worries about the King's blood pressure. The two often seem more like friendly rivals than ruler and subject. They seem to enjoy fighting about their differences and seeing who can predict the outcome of certain events. Although the Grand Duke is happy to boast when he is right, he is unlikely to kick up a fuss when he's wrong.

119

Jaq

Jaq is the leader of Cinderella's mouse friends. He is the one who finds Gus and tells Cinderella there is a new mouse in the house. He is also the first mouse to confront Lucifer and the only one willing to take the cat on. Jaq can be recognized by his orange jacket, red hat and turtleneck, and high-pitched voice. He is incredibly fond of Cinderella—or Cinderelly, as he calls her—and looks up to her like a mother or a big sister.

did you **know?**

- **Jaq's name is pronounced differently by different characters, with some calling him "Jock" or "Jack." He responds to them all equally.**

- **Jaq's high-pitched, rapid, almost unintelligible language was named "Mouse Latin" by Disney story man Winston Hibler.**

Gus

Gus, or Gus-Gus, as he's sometimes known, is Jaq's best friend. This chubby mouse is a bit dim-witted. Other than his friends, the most important thing to him is making sure his belly is full. This has been known to cause problems, and Gus has had more than one run-in with Lucifer. In fact, Gus is Lucifer's favorite target. The mean-spirited cat is sure the extra-plump mouse would make an extra-filling meal. Despite his easygoing demeanor, Gus is incredibly brave. He would do anything for Cinderella, even stand up to Lucifer.

Suzy

Suzy is the mother figure among Cinderella's mouse friends. It is her job to tuck the mice into their beds at night. Suzy is hardworking and incredibly good with needle and thread. She plays a big role in getting Cinderella's dress ready for the ball and is nearly as devastated as Cinderella herself when it is destroyed.

Prince Charming

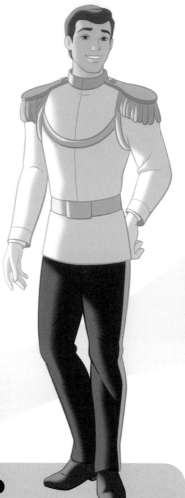

In spite of his power and royal status, the Prince is far from shallow. He judges people more by their personality and behavior than by their social standing. Still a young man, the Prince is not eager to marry. He is, in fact, downright rebellious when his father tells him it is time to settle down, and he only goes along with the ball because he has no other choice. Throughout the ball, he is seen to be yawning sarcastically, rolling his eyes, and glaring at his father. In spite of being surrounded by beautiful women who would happily be his princess, the Prince remains unimpressed by his prospects—at least until Cinderella shows up.

did you **know?**

- **The Prince is only on-screen for a little more than two minutes total. He was originally supposed to have a larger role, but artists found him too difficult to realistically animate.**

- **Not only is the Prince's real name never revealed, but he is never referred to as Prince Charming in the movie. He was called Prince Charming in the film's marketing materials and merchandise, and the name stuck!**

- **One early draft of the script featured a longer ending, including a solo song for the Prince.**

Miguel Rivera

Despite his family's generations-old ban on music, Miguel Rivera dreams of becoming an accomplished musician like his idol, Ernesto de la Cruz. Desperate to prove his talent, Miguel finds himself in the stunning and colorful Land of the Dead following a mysterious chain of events. Along the way, he meets charming trickster Héctor, and together, they set off on an extraordinary journey to unlock the real story behind Miguel's family history.

did you **know?**

- **Miguel comes from the town of Santa Cecilia, named after the patron saint of music.**

Mamá Coco

Miguel's great-grandmother Mamá Coco doesn't say much, but Miguel is eager to learn from her, the oldest living Rivera, about his family's past.

Dante

Nearly hairless and missing some teeth, Dante is a Xolo dog, short for Xoloitzcuintle, the national dog of Mexico. Dante becomes a loyal companion to Miguel and guides him on his adventure through the Land of the Dead.

Ernesto de la Cruz

Star of stage and screen, the charming and charismatic Ernesto de la Cruz is the most famous musician to ever come out of the town of Santa Cecilia. Even after his tragic death onstage during a live performance, de la Cruz is just as beloved in the Land of the Dead as he was in the Land of the Living.

Héctor

Héctor is a delightful and scrappy trickster who is on the verge of being completely forgotten by those in the Land of the Living. In a desperate effort to keep his memory alive, he makes a deal with a most unlikely companion—a human boy named Miguel, who finds himself in the Land of the Dead.

Mamá Imelda

Mamá Imelda is the matriarch of the Rivera family and Miguel's great-great-grandmother. Imelda was once the founder of the family's successful shoemaking business, which she used to support herself and her daughter after her musician husband left the family. Mamá Imelda becomes a spirit after her death, and when Miguel meets her, he learns a lot more about his family's past.

Abuelita Rivera

Abuelita (Elena) is Miguel's grandmother and the current matriarch of the Rivera family. She was raised to believe that music is a curse to her family, and that is one of the traditions she makes sure to pass down to the new generations. A second tradition she shares is the importance of family, particularly on Día de los Muertos.

Dumbo

Dumbo is a little elephant with *big* ears. More than anything, he loves being with his mother and grows incredibly upset when the two are separated. Luckily, Dumbo quickly finds a companion and best friend in Timothy Q. Mouse. Although initially scared of Timothy, Dumbo has a big heart and is able to look past the mouse's appearance and see him for what he is—a true friend. Just a baby, Dumbo is incredibly naive about the ways of the world. He doesn't realize when he is being made fun of or that the "magic feather" Timothy gives him isn't really magic. But Dumbo's trusting innocence is not altogether bad. It is his belief in the feather's magic, and later in himself, that allows him to use his ears to fly!

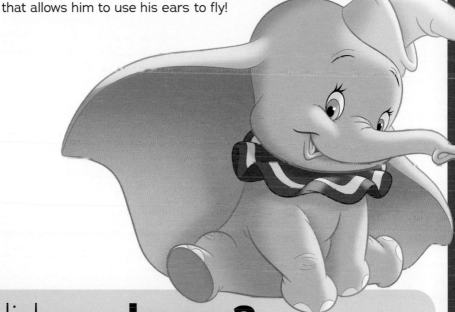

did you **know?**

- **Dumbo's real name is Jumbo Jr. He is given the nickname Dumbo by one of the other elephants.**

- **Dumbo is the only character in this movie who doesn't speak.**

- **With the exception of three hairs on the top of his head, Dumbo is completely hairless.**

Mrs. Jumbo

More than anything, Mrs. Jumbo wants a child. When the stork delivers Dumbo, she is absolutely thrilled. Although the other elephants laugh at Dumbo's big ears, Mrs. Jumbo doesn't care. To her, Dumbo is perfect. Tender, loving, and incredibly supportive, Mrs. Jumbo is everything a mother should be. She is also incredibly protective of her son. She cannot stand the thought of anyone being cruel to him or teasing him. When Dumbo becomes a star, Mrs. Jumbo beams with pride.

did you **know?**

- **Joe Grant and Dick Huemer changed Dumbo's mother's name from Mother Ella to Mrs. Jumbo as a reference to the famed Barnum & Bailey circus pachyderm.**

- **Her only speaking line in the film is when she names her son Jumbo Jr. Other than that, she remains completely silent.**

- **Mrs. Jumbo's eyes are blue. In real life, all elephants have brown eyes.**

Mr. Stork

Mr. Stork is a little bird with a big job: he has to deliver babies to their mothers. Mr. Stork is very organized and dutiful. He carries with him a map to make sure babies are going to the right place, and he would never dream of failing to deliver his loads successfully. Mr. Stork's most notable delivery is a little elephant named Dumbo to his mother, Mrs. Jumbo. Although he at first has trouble finding the elephants, he ultimately succeeds in getting the little bundle of joy to the right home.

Catty

Catty is a circus elephant. She lives for gossip, often being the one to bring news to the other elephants and share their news with the rest of the circus. Although not intentionally mean, Catty is certainly rather insensitive. She is the one who gives Dumbo his nickname. She does seem to know that her words could be hurtful, however, and sometimes spells them out so Dumbo won't understand what is being said about him. Catty is the third elephant to climb onto the Pyramid of Pachyderms.

Casey Jr.

A 2-4-0 steam engine with a tall smokestack, a short stumpy boiler, and a whistle on top, Casey Jr. is responsible for transporting the circus animals from place to place. Casey is a tenderhearted train. Although he is able to speak, he usually conveys his emotions by twisting and flexing his metal body. This gives him the ability to shrug and point, among other gestures.

The Ringmaster

Short-tempered and strict, the Ringmaster runs a tight ship. He is determined to put on a profitable show and make money for himself. Although not actually mean-spirited, the Ringmaster is incredibly ambitious. He wants the circus to be the best it can be, even if that means pushing the animals harder than may be good for them. But he is also open to trying new things, as he proves when he puts Dumbo into the clowns' act.

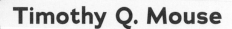

Timothy Q. Mouse

Timothy is nothing if not a true friend. His primary goal is to make Dumbo happy. Although small in stature, Timothy is a big presence at the circus. He is incredibly brave and will stand up to anyone in defense of Dumbo. He is also quite clever. He knows how to manipulate a situation to get what he wants, such as getting Dumbo into the circus or tricking his big-eared friend into thinking he can fly. Timothy acts not only as Dumbo's protector but as his manager and motivator, pushing him to be the best he can be.

The Clowns

The clowns take great pride in their job as the circus comedians. They are used to doing anything for a laugh and don't care who they humiliate in the process. As far as they are concerned, the only way to earn the respect of the audience is to earn their laughter, no matter what it takes. But the clowns are also easily scared. When they see Dumbo flying, they immediately run for cover, sure he will take revenge on them for humiliating him.

Kuzco

The self-centered emperor Kuzco believes that everyone is beneath him. He is sheltered and lacks common sense. He was raised by Yzma, his adviser, who ruled the kingdom for him as he grew up. Kuzco fires her for no reason, and she decides to get revenge on him by ordering her assistant, Kronk, to poison the emperor. But Kronk mistakes the bottle of poison for another one, and Kuzco turns into a llama! Kuzco goes on an adventure with Pacha to try to get himself turned back into a human so he can return home. Along the way, he learns humility, empathy, courage, and loyalty.

did you **know?**

- **Kuzco is seemingly ambidextrous. He writes with his right hand as a human and with his left hoof as a llama.**

- **Kuzco's name is derived from Cuzco, the name of a city in Peru that was the capital of the Inca Empire.**

Pacha

Pacha is a llama herder and the leader of a village. He is Tipo and Chaca's father and Chicha's husband. His hut sits on the highest of the village's hills, where the sun hits perfectly. Kuzco wants to knock down Pacha's home to build a summer palace, but Pacha will stop at nothing to defend his family's home. He cares very deeply for his family, and he will always do what's right for them and his people. After Kuzco turns back into a human, Pacha and his family allow the emperor to live in a summer hut right next door to their home.

Chicha

Chicha is Pacha's wife and Tipo and Chaca's mother. She loves Pacha deeply, and she is devoted to raising her children the right way. When Kuzco meets her, she is pregnant with her third child. She teaches Kuzco about family life.

Kronk

Kronk is Yzma's young and handsome right-hand man. Although he isn't very bright, he's an excellent chef and he oftentimes points out the flaws in Yzma's crazy and ridiculous plans. Also, he inadvertently turned Kuzco into a llama instead of poisoning him. While working for Yzma, Kronk often faces moral dilemmas, which lead to his imagining angel and devil versions of himself on his shoulders. He can talk to animals, and his best friend is Bucky the squirrel.

Yzma

Yzma raised Kuzco and acts as his adviser. She is hungry for power, and when Kuzco fires her, she plots revenge. Yzma thinks of herself as the most beautiful woman in the empire, even though she is quite old. She loves the color purple, and she often wears elaborate costumes. She commonly falls into fits of rage when things don't go her way. Her desire for power backfires on her when she drinks the wrong potion and turns into a kitten.

Nemo

Nemo is a curious and impressionable clownfish who lives alone with his overprotective single father, Marlin. Nemo has led a very sheltered life. He yearns for adventure and dreams of seeing the wonders of the Great Barrier Reef. Despite being born with one smaller, weaker fin, Nemo doesn't let anything hold him back. Unfortunately, his can-do attitude doesn't always have the best results. Determined to prove his bravery, Nemo swims out beyond the Drop-off—only to be caught by a scuba diver and taken to live in a tank at a dentist's office. It is only once he's been captured that Nemo learns the real meaning of bravery and comes to truly appreciate his father. These days, Nemo is happy to spend his time with Marlin and their friend Dory in the sea anemone he calls home— though he still enjoys a good adventure!

did you **know?**

- **Nemo makes a cameo in *Monsters, Inc.* as a toy in Boo's room.**

- **The name Nemo is Latin for "no one."**

Mr. Ray

Mr. Ray is Nemo's teacher. He believes in giving his students a practical, fins-on education. He often gives his students rides on his back to show them other creatures living in the ocean, and he sings songs to help them remember what they've learned. Although incredibly jolly and optimistic, Mr. Ray is also realistic. He recognizes danger when he sees it and has been known to shelter his students under his fins to protect them. Mr. Ray takes his teaching seriously and will happily answer any question his students may have—assuming he knows the answer.

Tad

One of Nemo's classmates, Tad is a yellow-and-purple butterfly fish. This little guy is rather obnoxious, and proud of it. He's also daring. When he and his friends see a boat off the edge of the Drop-off, they each take turns trying to swim as close to it as possible. But Tad's sense of adventure has its limits. When he sees a diver, he quickly swims away.

Sheldon

Sheldon is a classmate of Nemo's. Although the two are now friends, Sheldon initially made fun of Nemo for his small fin. He was scolded by his father for his behavior and has since been much kinder to Nemo. Like Nemo's other friends, Sheldon is brave, if immature. He joins the other students in seeing who can swim the farthest off the reef, but he quickly retreats when he sees the diver who ultimately takes Nemo. Life for Sheldon is a bit tough underwater, as the poor little sea horse is "H_2O intolerant."

Pearl

A little flapjack octopus, Pearl is another of Nemo's classmates and friends. Although Pearl joins her classmates in swimming off the reef, she quickly grows frightened. In fact, Pearl finds most things frightening. Whenever she is startled, she inks, releasing a black cloud into the ocean around her. According to Pearl, one of her tentacles is shorter than the other—although no one else can see the difference. She also claims to be able to walk on land.

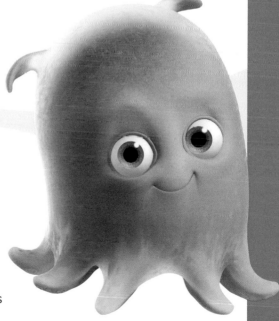

Marlin

As a young clownfish, Marlin was playful, happy, and easygoing. But everything changed when his wife and all but one of his children were eaten by a barracuda. Marlin swore in that moment to protect his one remaining child, and he has kept that promise. Over time, Marlin has grown incredibly serious. In spite of being a clownfish, he can't tell a good joke. Overprotective, paranoid, and worrisome, Marlin fears something bad happening to Nemo. The only way he knows to deal with this is to watch over Nemo so closely that nothing can happen to him. He even accompanies Nemo to his first day of school. Although he may go overboard in protecting his son, everything Marlin does is because he loves Nemo more than anything in the world. When he learns he must journey across the ocean to rescue Nemo, Marlin discovers his love is strong enough to overcome even his greatest fears. Along the way, Marlin also learns to lighten up, let go, and even accept help from others—particularly a blue tang fish named Dory, of whom he becomes incredibly fond.

did you **know?**

- **Marlin's wife's name was Coral. Before the barracuda appeared, the two were waiting for four hundred eggs to hatch!**

- **Marlin makes a cameo in *Monsters, Inc.* He can be seen in a painting hanging on the wall behind the sushi chef.**

Crush

When it comes to traveling the ocean's currents, no one has as much fun as Crush. This 150-year-old sea turtle is young at heart, with a laid-back surfer dude attitude that lets him go with the flow. But Crush is no drifter; he loves nothing more than the thrill of riding the rollicking East Australian Current with his son Squirt. Crush is a helpful guy. He happily helps Marlin and Dory get to Sydney Harbor to rescue Nemo and later helps Marlin, Nemo, and Dory get to California to find Dory's parents.

Squirt

Squirt is like a smaller version of his father. Equally laid-back, he loves riding the current and shares Crush's fearless attitude. Squirt's welcoming, high-spirited personality allows him to make friends anywhere. He enjoys playing hide-and-seek with Dory and even joins Nemo's class for a time as an exchange student.

Bruce

B ruce is a friendly and *usually* vegetarian great white shark. Bruce feels that sharks have gotten a bad rap and is out to fix his reputation. He is part of a nice-shark club of recovering meat-eaters whose motto is "fish are friends, not food." Although generally a laid-back guy who enjoys a good laugh, Bruce has little control over himself once his natural instincts kick in. At the smell of blood, he turns into a mindless fish-eating shark. Bruce is also very ticklish.

Anchor

A nchor is a vegetarian hammerhead shark who fights his instinct to eat fish every day. He's a nice guy, and he wants to be friends with the rest of the fish in the ocean—if only he can get over his nasty habit of eating them! He's smaller and thinner than the other sharks in his support group for recovering meat-eaters.

Dory

Nowhere in the ocean will you find a more welcoming, sociable, talkative fish than Dory. She would love to chat all day long and would gladly tell her life story to anyone who would listen—if she could just remember it. Dory is a blue tang fish with short-term memory loss. Although a few things stick with her (such as how to read English and speak Whale!), most information flies out of her head in a matter of seconds. She was separated from her parents as a child when she got caught in the undertow, and she

has only recently remembered them and been reunited with them. Being on her own for so long, Dory developed a bit of separation anxiety. Although she's actually quite capable of taking care of herself, she fears being left behind and forgetting everything she's managed to retain. Dory values her friendships and is an incredibly loyal friend. She does things her own way and inspires others to do the same.

did you **know?**

- **Dory was originally supposed to be a male character, but the writer of the movie was inspired when watching *The Ellen DeGeneres Show* and wrote the character specifically to be played by Ellen.**

- **Dory cannot remember Nemo's name. She instead calls him Chico, Fabio, Bingo, Harpo, Elmo, or Memo.**

Chum

Chum is a hyperactive mako shark with a hook lodged in his snout as a result of a fight with a fisherman. As a pup, Chum attended a posh boarding school for predators. These days he is part of the "fish are friends, not food" support group, although he does not seem entirely committed to the cause. Chum looks bored while reciting the club's pledge and admits to "misplacing" the fish friend he was supposed to bring to a meeting. Chum enjoys participating in shoving fights with fellow support-group member Anchor and has a particular dislike for dolphins.

Nigel

Nigel is a brown pelican who lives in Sydney Harbor. He spends the vast majority of his time in the window of a dentist's office, diagnosing dental problems with the help of his friends in the dentist's fish tank. Unfortunately for Nigel, the dentist is not particularly fond of having a pelican in his window and often chases him away. Nigel is a friendly guy, eager to help out others. He saves Marlin and Dory from an attack by some seagulls and brings them to the dentist's office to rescue Nemo.

Peach

Unless you are a starfish, you have no idea how slowly time can really pass. Stuck high up on the glass, Peach sees and broadcasts everything that goes on outside the tank—but nothing of interest ever happens. Peach has no option but to count tiles, memorize innumerable dental procedures, and then do it again . . . and again.

Gurgle

Gurgle is a colossal germophobe. If they made little rubber gloves for fish, he would be first in line to get them. Believing everything is covered with germs, Gurgle won't touch anything. He is terrified of his surroundings: the tank walls, the pebbles that cover the bottom, even the other fish. He knows the limited life expectancy of tank fish, and he is not taking any chances.

Gill

Gill is the maverick of the dentist's office fish tank. He is the leader of an eclectic group of tropical fish known as the Tank Gang, who hang on his every word and are drawn to his magnetic personality. This tough, scarred fish was raised in the ocean, but he was taken at a young age to live in a tank. Surrounded by fish who have spent their entire lives in "the box," Gill alone feels the pull to be free. Though he dreams of one day breaking out and returning to the ocean, his failed escape attempts have broken his spirit. With Nemo's arrival in the tank, Gill is inspired again to find a way back to the sea.

Bloat

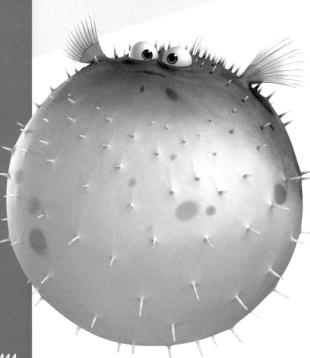

Bloat can blow up, and it's not just because he is a blowfish. He's got a temper. This temperamental character tries his best to maintain a sunny disposition. He is also Gill's trusted lieutenant in running tank business. However, the stress of being cooped up in a glass box with the other fish (especially Gurgle) is often more than he can handle, and he tends to *blow* things out of proportion.

Jacques

Every fish tank needs a creature to help clean the enclosed watery environment. In this tank it is Jacques, who cleans and cleans with the fervor of a soldier in the French Resistance— and also talks like one. Just yell his name and this little fighter races to do battle with his sworn enemy: tank scum.

Darla Sherman

Darla is the niece of the dentist. Although a bit bratty and spoiled, she is not intentionally mean to the fish. She is just a bit careless. Darla loves fish and is thrilled at the prospect of having one as a pet. But as any member of the Tank Gang will quickly note, she's not the best with them. In fact, her nickname is "Fish Killer." Darla gets so excited about the fish her uncle gives her that she has a tendency to shake the bags they are in . . . until the fish die. Nemo uses this trait to his advantage to escape the dentist's office.

Bubbles

Like a playful puppy obsessed with a favorite toy, Bubbles is enamored of bubbles. All day he faithfully waits for them to burst from the tank's plastic treasure chest and then he joyously scrambles to put them back. They are "his" bubbles and he has got to catch them all.

Deb and Flo

Deb and her identical "twin sister," Flo, are like two peas in a pod. They do everything together: swim, laugh, share secrets . . . They are a perfect match. It's for this reason that the rest of the Tank Gang does not have the heart to tell Deb that Flo is merely her reflection on the tank glass.

Hank

Hank is an octopus. Actually, he's a septopus. He lost a tentacle—along with his sense of humor—somewhere along the way. An accomplished escape artist with an uncanny ability to camouflage himself, Hank is the first to greet Dory when she arrives at the Marine Life Institute. But make no mistake: Hank isn't looking for a friend. He's looking for a ride on the transport truck to Cleveland, where he can live out a life of peaceful solitude. But in order to get on the truck, Hank needs the tag the scientists gave Dory. Sarcastic and grumpy as Hank may be, he isn't without a heart. In fact, he has three of them! And that means Hank can't help caring for Dory. He even risks his own freedom to help her find her parents.

did you **know?**

- **Hank's tentacles were designed separately from his body. When the animators tried to attach them, only seven fit. Later on, they decided to work the affliction into the script.**

- **Hank has fifty suckers per tentacle, for a total of three hundred and fifty suckers!**

Fluke and Rudder

Fluke and Rudder are a pair of lazy sea lions who were rehabilitated and released from the Marine Life Institute. Now they spend their days sleeping on a warm rock just outside the institute. They usually can't be bothered to move from their comfortable spot. The only thing that annoys them more than having their naps interrupted is dealing with that irritating sea lion, Gerald.

Gerald

Gerald is an offbeat sea lion who carries a green pail in his mouth. He is the runt of the litter. All he wants is his own place on Fluke and Rudder's rock—a goal he achieves, if only for a minute!

Charlie

Charlie likes to joke around, but nothing is more important to him than teaching his memory-challenged daughter how to survive. He loves his little "Kelpcake" and would do anything for her. In fact, Charlie seems to know something about memory loss. He tends to be a bit forgetful himself, often needing to be reminded of things and having his sentences finished by his wife.

Jenny

On the surface Jenny appears flighty and cheerful, but at her core she is formidable. She dispenses the wisdom that will come to both define and protect her daughter. Although a bit worrisome, Jenny is careful to keep a smile on her face for the sake of her family. She makes a point of praising her daughter and playing along with her husband's jokes. Jenny has often told Dory she is fond of purple shells. This is one memory that sticks with Dory and ultimately helps her reunite with her family.

Destiny

D estiny is the Marine Life Institute's rescued whale shark. As a youngster, Destiny communicated (in Whale, of course) with baby Dory through the institute's pipes, but when their communication suddenly stopped, she was convinced she'd never see her friend again. When a blue tang named Dory drops into Destiny's pool one day, Destiny is overjoyed to discover that her long-lost pipe pal has returned. Destiny isn't a very confident swimmer, as her poor eyesight makes navigating a bit challenging. But thanks to Dory and her neighbor Bailey, Destiny overcomes her fears and gains the confidence she needs to return to the ocean.

did you **know?**

- **Although Destiny can speak Whale, she isn't one. A whale shark is actually a kind of shark.**

Bailey

Bailey, the Marine Life Institute's rescued beluga whale, was brought into the institute with a head injury. Convinced that his echolocation abilities were damaged in the incident, Bailey refuses to exercise his natural talent even though the doctors agree there is nothing wrong with him. He spends his days in never-ending arguments with Destiny, his whale shark neighbor. These two know how to push each other's buttons and expose each other's insecurities. It's only when Dory arrives that Bailey is finally forced to tap into his abilities. It takes him a while to get going, but once he does, he's able to help Dory on her journey and generally save the day.

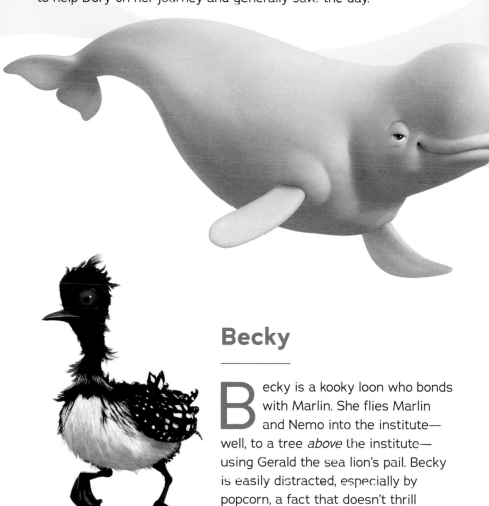

Becky

Becky is a kooky loon who bonds with Marlin. She flies Marlin and Nemo into the institute— well, to a tree *above* the institute— using Gerald the sea lion's pail. Becky is easily distracted, especially by popcorn, a fact that doesn't thrill Marlin. She also has a tendency to peck the people—or fish—she likes.

Big Mama

Big Mama is an owl who lives in the woods near Widow Tweed's home. She finds Tod as an orphaned pup and arranges his adoption by Widow Tweed. Big Mama possesses great wisdom. She often advises Tod, both as he's growing up and later when he's a mature fox. Loving and protective, Big Mama sees Tod as a son, even though she didn't raise him.

Widow Tweed

Widow Tweed is Tod's adoptive mother. The first time she sees Tod, she mentions feeling lonely after the loss of her husband. She takes Tod in, sure they can cure each other's loneliness. Widow Tweed is known for her kindness. Even when Tod is mischievous, she can't stay mad at him. She is also incredibly protective of the little fox. She happily stands up to the hunter Amos Slade and defends Tod's actions. But Widow Tweed knows she cannot protect the fox forever. Shortly after his first birthday, she decides to release him into a wilderness preserve, where he will be safe from hunters like Slade.

Tod

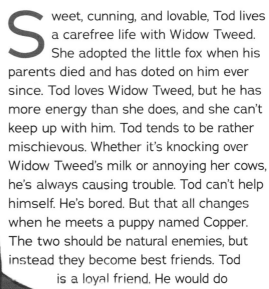

Sweet, cunning, and lovable, Tod lives a carefree life with Widow Tweed. She adopted the little fox when his parents died and has doted on him ever since. Tod loves Widow Tweed, but he has more energy than she does, and she can't keep up with him. Tod tends to be rather mischievous. Whether it's knocking over Widow Tweed's milk or annoying her cows, he's always causing trouble. Tod can't help himself. He's bored. But that all changes when he meets a puppy named Copper. The two should be natural enemies, but instead they become best friends. Tod is a loyal friend. He would do anything for Copper—and he does, helping him fight off an enormous bear. Unfortunately, Copper's master is not a fan of Tod, and the two must keep their friendship a secret.

did you **know?**

- **Although Tod is usually shown as a baby in merchandise, he actually has more screen time as an adult.**

- **The "glove" on Tod's right foreleg is longer than the one on his left.**

Amos Slade

Amos Slade is a crabby, grumpy, bad-tempered hunter. Professionally, Amos is a chicken farmer. His land is next to Widow Tweed's, a fact that annoys him to no end, since he can't seem to keep her pesky fox, Tod, off his property. Amos is unaware of Tod's friendship with Copper and believes the fox is after his chickens. He even threatens to kill Tod the next time he comes onto his land. But Amos is not all bad. He has a soft side for his dogs, Copper and Chief, and even shows remorse for trying to hurt Tod when the fox saves him from a dangerous bear.

Chief

Chief is an old Irish wolfhound. He is Amos Slade's pet and it shows. Like his master, Chief is mean, with a short temper. Chief wants nothing to do with Copper when the puppy first arrives on the farm, but Copper's playfulness and persistence finally win over the old hound. Chief takes Copper under his wing and teaches him everything he knows about being a hunting dog. In spite of his fondness for Copper, Chief never grows to like Tod. He urges Copper to put an end to their friendship and even joins Amos in trying to get rid of the fox once and for all.

Copper

Copper is one of two dogs owned by hunter Amos Slade. The other is Chief. Copper is meant to be a hunting dog. As such, he has an excellent sense of smell. That combined with natural puppy curiosity makes him prone to wandering off. It is on one of Copper's many excursions that he meets and befriends Tod. Copper is a kind, loving, loyal friend. He loves nothing more than to play with his best friend. But as he grows up, he comes to recognize the challenge of a hunter being friends with his prey, and he eventually turns away from Tod. Although their friendship is later rekindled, Copper has grown up. He takes his job as a hunting dog seriously and knows the friendship will never be the same.

did you **know?**

- **Copper's name changes in foreign versions of** *The Fox and the Hound*. **In Spain and Italy, he is known as Toby.**

- *The Fox and the Hound* **is based on a book of the same name. In the book, Copper is a coonhound/bloodhound mix. In the film he is just a coonhound.**

Vixey

Vixey is a forest fox. She grew up in the wild and has the survival skills to prove it. Big Mama thinks Vixey would make the perfect mate for Tod, and Vixey agrees—once the two actually begin to get along. Vixey and Tod get off to a rocky start, but they soon manage to smooth things over once Tod admits that he doesn't know how to make it in the forest. Vixey teaches Tod how to survive and becomes his mate. Caring and romantic, Vixey would like to be a mother someday. She thinks six little foxes would be the perfect number.

Dinky and Boomer

Dinky and Boomer are a sparrow and a woodpecker, respectively. They are Big Mama's assistants in the forest. Whether finding Tod a home with Widow Tweed or helping the fox realize that things will be different between him and Copper once they grow up, the two are there to help Big Mama put her plans into action. Dinky is small but brainy, while Boomer is strong, if a bit dim-witted. When not helping Big Mama, the two spend most of their time trying to catch a caterpillar named Squeaks. Unfortunately for them, they never manage to catch Squeaks, who transforms into a butterfly and flies away.

Elsa

Regal and composed, Elsa has the unusual power to create snow and ice. She used to be afraid of her power and its potential to hurt others. In fact, she spent most of her life squelching her emotions in order to hide her power from others. But all that has changed, thanks to the love and acceptance of her sister, Anna. These days, Elsa is happy and content in the Enchanted Forest as the fifth spirit, while her sister is queen of Arendelle. But Elsa is still happy to join the gang at the castle for the occasional game of charades.

did you **know?**

- **The head of Elsa's animated model has more than four hundred thousand individual strands of hair.**

- **An early version of the script for *Frozen* had Elsa as the villain of the movie.**

- **Elsa was born on the winter solstice.**

Anna

Anna is an idealist and an eternal optimist. She expects the best from every situation and displays an unshakable faith in others. Anna wears her heart on her sleeve. She is incredibly compassionate and is not shy about showing others how she feels. Above all, Anna is a doer. Having spent years locked behind the walls of the castle, watching the world pass her by, she jumps at the opportunity for adventure. And now that she is queen of Arendelle, she is happy to have the love of all her people—especially her new fiancé, Kristoff.

did you **know?**

- **One of Anna's favorite desserts is krumkake—a thin waffle-like cookie shaped like an ice-cream cone and stuffed with sweet fillings.**

- **Anna was born on the summer solstice.**

- **Anna is left-handed.**

- **Anna plays a mean game of charades—especially when she's playing with Elsa, Olaf, and Kristoff.**

King Agnarr

King Agnarr is a happy but very protective father and king. He loves his daughters and wants nothing more than to protect them from harm. King Agnarr does his best to teach Elsa to control her powers. It is from him that Anna and Elsa learn self-restraint and what it means to be a good leader. When King Agnarr was a boy, he went to the Enchanted Forest with his father. When the battle broke out between the Northuldra and the Arendellians, a young Northuldra girl saved him and left him outside the forest.

Queen Iduna

Queen Iduna is Anna and Elsa's mother. As queen of Arendelle, she is a great ruler. But her chief responsibility is to her daughters. Iduna loves them dearly and would do anything to protect them—especially from the secrets of her past. But as Elsa's powers continue to grow, Iduna wonders if her past might hold the answers for her family. Unfortunately, Queen Iduna and King Agnarr were lost in the Dark Sea while searching for these answers.

Kristoff

Kristoff may be a little bit of a fixer-upper, but this former ice harvester has a heart of gold—especially when he isn't lost in the woods. He grew up in the mountains of Arendelle, where he was raised by trolls. Having been orphaned at a young age, Kristoff is a realist with a practical view of the world. He knows how valuable family and friends are, and understands the importance of being true to oneself. Kristoff has never had to look out for anyone but himself and his reindeer, Sven—but that changed when he met Anna and Olaf. Now he is ready to take the next step with Anna as she tackles her new role as queen of Arendelle.

did you **know?**

- **Kristoff's full name is Kristoff Bjorgman.**

- **Kristoff mined the stone for Anna's engagement ring by himself out of the Black Mountains.**

Gerda

Gerda has been a servant in the castle since King Agnarr and Queen Iduna's reign. In fact, when the gates are closed, she is one of very few to remain in the castle. But Gerda is much more than just a servant. She is like a member of the family. It is her job to keep the royal household running.

Kai

Kai oversees the castle. He is much more than a staff member—he is more like a member of the family. It is Kai who informs Anna that her parents have passed and who helps Elsa prepare for her coronation. He also handles relations with the visiting dignitaries once the castle gates are reopened.

Sven

Sven is more than just the reindeer that pulls Kristoff's sleigh. He is also a loyal friend, at times even acting as a conscience for Kristoff. With a shake of his head or a stomp of his hoof, Sven can steer Kristoff onto the right track and keep him on his best behavior. Sven and Kristoff have conversations on a regular basis. Sure, Kristoff provides Sven's silly reindeer voice, but that doesn't make the conversations any less meaningful. Although Kristoff has now found the love of his life, he still leans on Sven to help him deal with his emotions. And Sven's heroism shows us once again why reindeer are better than people.

did you **know?**

- **Sven's favorite snacks are carrots and lichen.**
- **Sven was originally going to have only one antler.**
- **Sven's behavior is based off that of a dog.**

Bulda

In addition to nurturing the younger trolls, Bulda is Kristoff's adoptive mother. She loves Kristoff and wants what is best for him. In fact, Bulda is somewhat of a love expert. She is quite knowledgeable in the art of relationships and matchmaking, and feels that Anna is an excellent fit for her Kristoff.

Grand Pabbie

As old as the oldest rocks, Grand Pabbie is the wisest of the trolls. It is he who heals Anna when she is struck by Elsa's magic as a child and who warns Elsa that fear will be her enemy. It is also to Grand Pabbie whom Kristoff brings Anna when she is again struck by Elsa's magic. When a powerful magic threatens Arendelle, Grand Pabble brings news that Elsa's powers have awoken a most powerful and ancient magic. Grand Pabbie volunteers to take care of the villagers of Arendelle as Anna and Elsa depart on their journey to the Enchanted Forest.

Hans

Prince Hans of the Southern Isles is everything a prince should be: romantic, well educated, and smooth. On the surface, he appears to be Anna's knight in shining armor. But in reality there is nothing wholesome about this prince. As the youngest of thirteen brothers, Hans stands no chance of inheriting a kingdom on his own. He proposes to Anna the first day they meet, but he is motivated by greed rather than love. He wants a throne and is willing to go to any lengths to get it. Luckily, his scheme is revealed, and he is sent back to the Southern Isles.

did you **know?**

- **Hans's horse's name is Sitron.**
- **Hans has more siblings than any other Disney villain.**

Oaken

Oaken is the owner of Wandering Oaken's Trading Post and Sauna. He is good-natured and helpful, though he may throw you out in the snow if you offend him. Oaken is a true businessman. He recognizes the laws of supply and demand, so when a snowstorm overtakes Arendelle, he happily offers a deep discount on his summer items while doubling the price of the winter gear. He also fancies himself an amateur inventor. He sells many things of his own invention, including a sun balm and a cold remedy! Above all, Oaken is a family man. He cares deeply about his large family.

Duke of Weselton

The Duke of Weselton may have some impressive dance moves, but he's a weasel when it comes to trade. Arrogant and opportunistic, the Duke visits Arendelle hoping to find information he can exploit for his own profit. Ruled by fear, the Duke of Weselton proclaims Elsa a monster when her powers are revealed, and he tries to turn the people of Arendelle against their queen. Thankfully, the Duke is proven wrong when Elsa returns home and restores summer to Arendelle. As a result of his actions, all trade between Weselton and Arendelle is suspended.

Olaf

In summer or not, Olaf is one happy snowman. The first time Elsa and Anna built a snowman together, when they were children, was a moment of pure happiness. When Elsa later inadvertently creates a living snowman named Olaf, the happiness of that childhood moment is reflected in his personality. Olaf views the world with childlike naïveté and wonder. He sees the good in everything and rarely notices when things go wrong. Even in the face of grave danger, Olaf remains optimistic. While Olaf still loves warm hugs, he has also learned to read, and his questions have gotten bigger and more philosophical. He can also play a mean game of charades.

did you **know?**

- **Olaf no longer needs his personal flurry; Elsa has now given him a layer of permafrost!**

- **In order to accurately animate Olaf's walk cycle to mimic the way a child would move, one of Olaf's supervising animators used his son as a reference during production.**

- **Olaf is not able to bend his arms.**

Marshmallow

Back when she was secluded in the ice palace, Elsa created this giant ice guard to make sure people would leave her alone. Marshmallow, as he was named by Olaf, is a harmless mound of snow and ice until he gets angry. That's when the icicle spikes come out! These days, the big snowman lives in Elsa's ice palace, where he takes care of the snowgies . . . and keeps them out of trouble.

The Snowgies

These happy, energetic snowmen are the result of Elsa's first cold. Every time she sneezed, more of them would pop into the air. Snowgies love birthday cake—they will do anything to get a piece! Olaf loves them and calls them his little brothers. The snowgies live in Elsa's ice palace with Marshmallow.

Yelana

Yelana is the outspoken leader of the Northuldra, yet she resists seeing the similarities between them and the Arendellians. She is very protective of her people. She longs for the days when they were still in harmony with all of the spirits of nature. She is a firm believer that the Arendellians were the instigators of the battle, the day the mist surrounded the Enchanted Forest.

Honeymaren

Bold and brave, Honeymaren longs to roam the land with all of the reindeer, to be free of the conflicts of the past and the Enchanted Forest. When she meets Anna and Elsa, she is hopeful they might be the ones to finally help everyone escape from the Enchanted Forest. Honeymaren realizes that at their heart, the Arendellians and the Northuldra are far more alike than they are different.

Ryder

Ryder is Honeymaren's brother. He embraces life with gusto and handles tension with a disarming smile and a witty remark. Ryder's love of reindeer might just rival Kristoff's. In Kristoff he finds a kindred spirit—someone who knows what reindeer are thinking, and speaks for them, too! But unlike Kristoff, Ryder's never been able to roam the great plains or see the wide-open skies. He yearns to be set free of the Enchanted Forest and to embrace the world and all of the reindeer in it.

King Runeard

King Agnarr's father, Runeard is the grandfather of Elsa and Anna and the former king of Arendelle. He was ruler when Arendelle Castle and the village of Arendelle were built along Arenfjord. He built a dam to connect the lands of Northuldra as a symbol of peace. He also hosted a celebration for the Arendellians and Northuldra once the dam was completed. However, the king was lost at the same celebration when a battle of unknown origins broke out between the two groups of people.

Mattias

For years, Lieutenant Destin Mattias loyally protected his homeland of Arendelle and served as the official guard to Prince Agnarr. Although at times, he was more like the prince's wise older brother. But he became stuck in the Enchanted Forest, where he's been for more than thirty years. He's never forgotten his sworn duty to Arendelle, but the arrival of Elsa and discovery that she has a magical power is just the first of many challenges to his long-held beliefs. One thing he holds tight to is the advice given to him over the years by his beloved father.

FROZEN

Wind Spirit

Full of mischief, Gale is the first spirit encountered by our group from Arendelle. At first, it seems playful as it pulls everyone into its swirling vortex. But then it tightens tighter and tighter on Elsa, forcing Elsa to use her power in a new way.

Water Spirit

The mythical Water Nokk takes the form of a horse. It has the power of the ocean with the charge of a stallion, and can be found in any body of water in the Enchanted Forest, as well as in the depths of the Dark Sea. The Water Nokk is a fierce warrior and guards the secrets of the Enchanted Forest fiercely. A person must prove themselves worthy and earn its respect, before the Water Nokk will let them pass to discover the biggest secret of them all.

Fire Spirit

The Fire Spirit, named Bruni, appears during times of unrest. As the salamander runs around, it leaves a trail of fire in its wake. But the fire is not an ordinary one. It does not go out when Elsa blasts it with her power. It is only when the salamander crawls onto Elsa's palm and is calmed that all the flames go out.

Earth Giants

Asleep by day, Earth Giants roam the south end of the Enchanted Forest by night. They rise as tall as the trees and can flatten anything that stands in their way with one well placed foot or an expertly aimed boulder. They have a nose for the scent of Elsa's magic, and seek it out from wherever they are. But even when they rest, travelers on the river still need to be wary. What might seem like ordinary hills and mountains along the banks, are actually the sleeping giants.

Arlo

The runt of a family of strapping Apatosaurus dinosaurs, ten-year-old Arlo has grown up fearful of the world around him. Where Poppa sees beauty, Arlo only sees things to fear. Arlo wants to do his part to help out on the family farm, but his fear always gets in the way. When Arlo accidentally falls into a river and is swept hundreds of miles downstream, he finds himself far from home in a land filled with rough terrain and predatory animals. Alone, Arlo must learn to face his fears or risk never finding his way home. On the long and arduous journey back to his family's farm, Arlo develops an unexpected friendship with a strange creature he names Spot—a relationship that will help him realize he is capable of much more than he ever dreamed.

did you **know?**

- **Concept art for Arlo showed him as much larger than he is in the final film. He also had blue eyes and a light yellow snout.**

- **A toy of Arlo can be seen on the floor of one of the scare simulators in *Monsters University*.**

- **An early draft of the script had Arlo and his family as Amish-like dinosaurs.**

Poppa

Poppa is a devoted husband and father. He works hard to make the family farm a success and provide a good life for his wife and three children. Poppa is especially fond of Arlo, his smallest child, whom he takes special care of. Poppa nurtures and believes in his son. He knows Arlo can overcome any fear or doubt with the right amount of perseverance. He tries to show Arlo that the world is beautiful, not scary. Poppa dies saving Arlo from a flash flood.

Momma

A loving wife and mother, Momma is smart and quick-witted. She knows how important it is to keep the family farm running smoothly and gives it her all, especially after Poppa's death. Momma is the backbone of the family. She inspires her children to work hard and do their best. Momma is supportive of Arlo's determination to keep Poppa's spirit alive.

Spot

Spot is a feral human boy who has lived alone in the wilderness for the majority of his life. Spot speaks only in grunts, growls, and howls. Although he can't hold an intelligible conversation with Arlo, Spot nevertheless manages to get his meaning across. He is intelligent, fearless, confident, and resourceful. Spot once had a family, but they died when he was quite young. Spot quickly realizes Arlo is worthy of his trust and becomes a fiercely loyal ally.

did you **know?**

- **Early concept art of Spot shows him with a different hairstyle and dark brown eyes.**

Buck

Buck is Arlo's brother. Buck finds Arlo frustrating. He does not understand why Arlo is so frightened, and he grows annoyed with Arlo's always interrupting his chores. Buck is physically the largest of the three dino children. He is also the feistiest. His physical size, strength, and confidence allow him to do things that Arlo cannot . . . like rip a tree out of the ground with his teeth. Although Buck enjoys teasing his brother about his smaller size and general fearfulness, he does love him.

Libby

Arlo's sister, Libby, is a bit of a trickster. She's always playing silly pranks on her family. But when it comes to farm work, Libby pulls her weight. She can plow a mean field and helps bring in the crops. Although Libby sometimes comes off as a bit of a girly girl, she can be as rough-and-tumble as her brother Buck.

Butch

A rugged T. rex with a gruesome scar across his face, Butch is a brawny and intimidating rancher: a longhorn rustler's worst nightmare. But he is also an incredibly loyal friend and is always true to his word. If he promises you something, he'll deliver—as long as you do your part. A veteran rancher with years of experience herding longhorns, Butch has two children: Ramsey and Nash. He is teaching them the family business, hurling them into hairy situations and letting them find out what they're really made of. Butch likes nothing better than trading stories over a campfire at the end of a long day. Just ask him about the time he fought three crocodiles!

did you **know?**

- **When Butch grins, his teeth resemble the mustache of his voice actor, Sam Elliott.**

- **Butch fought and won against three crocs. He wears one of their teeth stuck in his gums as a souvenir.**

Ramsey

Ramsey is a T. rex rancher. She loves the challenge of driving home a herd of longhorns next to her father, Butch, and her little brother, Nash. Loud and outgoing, Ramsey loves hearing a good joke or telling a story. But she has a quiet side, too, and has been known to have a soft spot for those in need. She particularly takes a shine to Spot. Ramsey's little brother drives her nuts with his teasing, but mess with him at your peril: Ramsey is incredibly protective of Nash. The only thing she likes more than driving longhorns is a good fight—and she's got the scars to prove it!

Nash

An enthusiastic young T. rex, Nash lives for adventure. As much as he enjoys driving cattle with his father and sister, he loves when something unexpected breaks up the routine of rounding up longhorns. Nash isn't the sharpest of spurs and is easily distracted—so much so that he actually manages to lose an entire herd of longhorns! But Nash's mischievous charm and relaxed, positive attitude make him good company on a long cattle drive. Nash is also excellent at providing entertainment on those long nights. Whether it's his soulful bug-harmonica playing or a tall tale, he'll keep you mesmerized.

The Pet Collector

The Pet Collector is a fearful and mysterious Styracosaurus. He lives in the wilderness, blending into his surroundings of leaves and brush. Over the years, he has collected a number of small forest creatures. They now live on his horns and offer advice and observations to help keep him safe. The Pet Collector has a strong desire to add Arlo's human companion, Spot, to his collection of creatures, especially after he witnesses Spot defending Arlo from a snakelike creature.

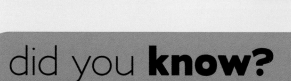

did you **know?**

- **Each of the animals living on the Pet Collector's horns serve a purpose. Fury (a sloth-like creature) protects him from creatures that crawl in the night. Destructor (a furry fox critter) protects him from mosquitoes. Dreamcrusher (a cute big-eyed walrus creature) protects him from having unrealistic goals. And Debbie (a kooky red bird) serves as his most trusted ally.**

The Pterodactyls

These winged scavengers pose a great threat to Arlo and Spot during their journey through the wilderness. Overly enthusiastic storm chasers, the Pterodactyls credit storms with inspiring them and giving them their unique names. The Pterodactyls appear after bad storms, like a search and rescue team. But they aren't out to rescue anyone. Instead, they are scavenging through the wreckage of the storm for a good meal. Although they offer to help Spot and Arlo, they quickly turn vicious when Arlo refuses to give Spot to them.

The Raptors

Also known as rustlers, these feathered, dim-witted Raptors prey on the T. rexes' herd of longhorns. Though he's the leader of the pack, Bubbha is not exactly bright, and his brother Pervis is quite dumb. Earl may be the quietest of the thieves, but he sure is tough and mean. Lurleane always steals the show with her crazy antics. Despite being much smaller than the T. rexes, the Raptors pose a serious threat, especially as a group.

Basil of Baker Street

Basil of Baker Street is a brilliant mouse investigator, also known as the Great Mouse Detective. Basil lives on Baker Street, in the home of Sherlock Holmes, and models his life after the famous detective's. Basil is determined to beat his nemesis, Professor Ratigan, at all costs. He can be very self-centered. In fact, when he first meets Olivia Flaversham and Dr. Dawson, he barely acknowledges them. It is only when he realizes that taking Olivia's case will lead him to Ratigan that he agrees to help. Basil is a genius with a multitude of different areas of expertise, including history, science, and disguise.

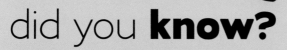

did you **know?**

- **Basil's name draws inspiration from that of Basil Rathbone, an actor who portrayed Sherlock Holmes numerous times.**

Olivia Flaversham

Olivia Flaversham seeks out the Great Mouse Detective after her father, Hiram Flaversham, is abducted by a peg-legged bat named Fidget. Olivia is a very brave young mouse and is determined to find her father. She even helps the detective locate Hiram. Unfortunately, she is also kidnapped by Fidget, and Basil must save her.

Hiram Flaversham

Hiram Flaversham is Olivia's father and the best mouse toymaker in all of London. Unfortunately, being the best is not always a good thing, because his extreme skill draws the attention of Professor Ratigan, who kidnaps him to create a clockwork mouse queen. Hiram refuses at first, but when Ratigan threatens Olivia's life, Hiram agrees to finish the invention. Hiram is rescued by Basil and Dr. Dawson, but his inventing days are not over. When he hears that Olivia has been kidnapped, Hiram creates a balloon ship to save her.

Dr. Dawson

Dr. Dawson is a highly respected mouse surgeon who has recently traveled to Afghanistan in service of the queen. Upon his return to England, he immediately runs into a crying Olivia. Dr. Dawson helps Olivia find the great Basil of Baker Street and assists the great detective in finding Olivia's father, Hiram. Dr. Dawson's bumbling personality and heart of gold complement Basil's shrewd detective skills. The two mice work very well together. After they rescue Hiram and Olivia, defeat Ratigan, and save the queen, Basil takes on Dr. Dawson as his partner.

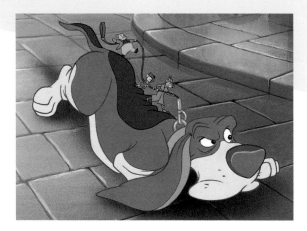

Toby

Sherlock Holmes's friendly basset hound, Toby, has the most splendid sense of smell. Even though he belongs to Mr. Holmes, he is eager to help with Basil's detective work. Toby's strong nose makes him excellent at tracking down thieves, although his frisky nature makes working with him a bit risky. Toby is massive compared to the mice he works with, and he has been known to accidentally step on them. But Toby means no harm. Overall, he is one incredibly friendly pup.

Professor Ratigan

Professor Ratigan is Basil of Baker Street's archrival. He is a large rat with gray fur who often wears dark suits with a long black cape. Ratigan hates being called a rat and is prone to fits of violence. He is charismatic but cold, calculating, and manipulative. He appears to be a gentleman but has many sinister motives. Ratigan has a number of henchmen to do his bidding, including Fidget the bat, Felicia the cat, and Bill the lizard. Ratigan plots to take over Mousedom by replacing Queen Moustoria with a robot so he can make himself king. He orders Fidget to kidnap Hiram and Olivia as part of his plan. But Ratigan is thwarted by Basil of Baker Street, and the villain falls off the Big Ben clock tower to his doom.

did you **know?**

- **In the novels the film was based on, Ratigan is actually a mouse, despite his name. This was changed for the film.**

Fidget

Fidget is a peg-legged bat with a poor ability to fly. He is also Professor Ratigan's right-hand man. In spite of his inability to fly well, Fidget is incredibly cunning and stealthy and is able to pull off many heists for Ratigan. In particular, he kidnaps Hiram Flaversham and, later, Olivia. But Fidget is very forgetful and clumsy and often accidentally leaves things behind. These clues allow Basil to track down Professor Ratigan.

Queen Moustoria

Queen Moustoria is the queen of Mousedom. The queen is kidnapped by Professor Ratigan before her sixty-year jubilee and then rescued by Olivia's dog friend Toby. Toby saves the queen from being eaten by Ratigan's cat, Felicia. Queen Moustoria is very grateful to Basil, Toby, Olivia, Hiram, and Dr. Dawson for saving her and the kingdom from Ratigan's evil plot, even going so far as to bestow knighthood on Basil and Dr. Dawson.

Hercules

Hercules has never felt like he belongs, and his unexplained superstrength has always gotten him into trouble. When his parents finally reveal the truth to him—that they found him wearing the medallion of Zeus and raised him as their own—he sets off to seek answers. Hercules finds out he is the son of Zeus and decides he must prove himself as a hero so he can join his parents on Mount Olympus. Hercules is very compassionate and innocent; he wants to protect others. He falls in love with Meg at first sight and helps the gods overthrow Hades and the Titans. It is on this mission that Hercules learns his greatest lesson: a true hero isn't measured by his physical strength but by the strength of his heart. Instead of becoming a god and rejoining his parents on Mount Olympus, he chooses to give up his immortality to live with Meg and his friends as a mortal.

did you **know?**

- **Despite being the son of the king and queen of the gods, Hercules is not considered an official Disney prince.**

- **Hercules is one of the few characters in the movie who goes by his Roman name. The majority of the gods use their Greek names.**

Hades

This god of the Underworld is quite literally a hothead. He has an uncontrollable temper, and his blue-flamed hair turns red-hot when he's angry. Hades hates the Underworld and wants nothing more than to take the throne on Mount Olympus from his brother Zeus. He is often cruel to the souls who inhabit the Underworld. In fact, his chief minions are named Pain and Panic. Hades loves to make deals; he is a master manipulator, but he honors every bargain he strikes. Hades's love of deals is eventually his undoing. In exchange for Hercules's strength, Hades promises that Meg will not be hurt. But Meg sacrifices herself for Hercules and is gravely injured. Hercules gets his strength back and throws Hades into a river of death.

did you **know?**

- **Originally, Hades was going to be portrayed as a more serious villain. It wasn't until James Woods auditioned for the role that Hades was rewritten as a comic-relief villain with a huge sense of humor.**

The Hydra

The Hydra is a large reptilian monster with three gruesome snakelike heads. Any time one head gets cut off, another three grow in its place. The Hydra is the first monster Hades sends to fight Hercules outside the city of Thebes. Hercules is able to overcome the monster by using his strength to cause a rockslide that crushes the beast.

Nessus

This large centaur—half horse, half man—is also known as the River Guardian. Hades sends Meg to try to recruit Nessus for his army, but the centaur takes Meg captive. Despite Meg's insistence that she doesn't need help, Hercules comes to her rescue and defeats Nessus.

Philoctetes

This satyr—half man and half goat—goes by Phil. He has a big heart but also a fiery temper. He does not like being ignored or disrespected and is immediately suspicious of Meg. He's trained heroes for years and has always dreamed of training one so great that the gods will hang a picture of the hero in the stars and people will know "that's Phil's boy!" Phil gets his wish with Hercules.

did you **know?**

- **Although Phil and Hades are aware of each other, the two never interact.**

- **Prior to training Hercules, Phil trained Achilles.**

Pegasus

Pegasus is Hercules's winged horse and his best friend. Zeus created Pegasus when Hercules was just a baby. Pegasus is very protective of Hercules and will never hesitate to jump into battle and fly to his aid. Pegasus also can be very jealous of sharing his best friend's attention with anyone else. He does not like it when Hercules starts spending a lot of time with Meg. Pegasus is by Hercules's side through thick and thin and helps the demigod defeat Hades.

Megara

Megara, Meg for short, is no damsel in distress. She's sharp and cynical and can take care of herself. Hercules falls in love with her at first sight. Meg sold her soul to Hades in exchange for her boyfriend's life, but her boyfriend abandoned her. She's a reluctant prisoner of Hades and initially goes along with his schemes to undermine Hercules. But she tries to stop once she realizes that she has feelings for the handsome demigod. She pushes Hercules out of the way of a falling pillar and is crushed. Hercules defeats Hades and goes to the Underworld to save Meg's soul. Hercules chooses a life with Meg over being a god, and the two live a happy mortal life together.

Esmeralda

Esmeralda is a beautiful Romany woman. Cunning and street-smart, she lives on the streets of Paris with her pet goat, Djali. Esmeralda is no damsel in distress, and she has no problem taking care of herself. At the Festival of Fools, she outwits many of Frollo's soldiers and thugs. She even saves Phoebus's life after he is injured by Frollo, and the two slowly fall in love. Esmeralda is kind and compassionate, a champion for the poor and downtrodden. It is she who stands up to Frollo and stops the crowd from throwing food at Quasimodo. Quasimodo saves Esmeralda from Frollo, and in return she shows him the goodness in the world that he's been missing out on for so long.

did you **know?**

- **Esmeralda lives underneath Paris, France, in the hidden catacombs known as the Court of Miracles.**

Quasimodo

Quasimodo is the bell ringer of Notre Dame. He has lived his entire life inside the cathedral, under the watchful eye of Judge Claude Frollo, who forbids Quasimodo to leave the tower. Despite Frollo's claims that people will be cruel to Quasimodo because he has a hunchback, Quasimodo yearns to explore the world and spends much of his time imagining what life would be like down below. He is a talented artist and creates a miniature replica of Notre Dame, its surroundings, and the townspeople. Quasimodo is extremely agile and strong from ringing the bells. Despite the cruelty he's been shown his whole life, Quasimodo is kind and innocent, often nursing baby birds back to health. When he decides to attend the Festival of Fools, his whole world is turned topsy-turvy. He meets the beautiful Esmeralda, who is the first person ever to be kind to him. She defends him when the festival takes a violent turn, and the two become friends when she claims sanctuary in Notre Dame. After the siege of Notre Dame, Esmeralda leads him to the outside world, where the townspeople welcome him and accept him for who he is—a hero.

did you **know?**

- **Quasimodo's parents were Romanies.**
- **Quasimodo is about twenty years old.**
- **Quasimodo has green eyes.**

Hugo

Hugo is the most fun of Quasimodo's three gargoyle best friends. He often cracks jokes, and he is always the first to suggest breaking Frollo's rules if it means bringing Quasimodo happiness. He loves entertainment and romance. Along with Laverne and Victor, he is one of Quasimodo's biggest supporters.

The Archdeacon

The Archdeacon is a devout clergyman at the Notre Dame cathedral in Paris. He saved Quasimodo from Frollo when the hunchback was a baby by reminding the evil judge that he could not run from his eventual judgment from God. The Archdeacon cannot stand to see injustice done, and he stands up for Esmeralda when she seeks sanctuary from Frollo in Notre Dame. The Archdeacon takes sanctuary seriously and will see no one come to harm on his watch or in his cathedral.

Laverne

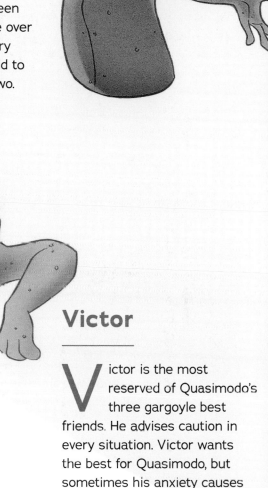

Laverne is the oldest and wisest of Quasimodo's three gargoyle best friends. She often gives Quasimodo motherly advice, and she acts as the voice of reason between Hugo and Victor, who can be over the top. She also has her fiery moments, and she isn't afraid to use a well-placed insult or two.

Victor

Victor is the most reserved of Quasimodo's three gargoyle best friends. He advises caution in every situation. Victor wants the best for Quasimodo, but sometimes his anxiety causes him to burst into sobbing fits.

Phoebus

Phoebus is Frollo's captain of the guard. Phoebus returned from the wars to command Frollo's guard, but he disagrees with Frollo's ideas of justice. He helps Esmeralda escape from some of Frollo's thugs, and his feelings for her grow over time. When Phoebus refuses to burn down an innocent family's house and instead risks his own life to save the family, Frollo orders his soldiers to open fire on the captain. Phoebus later rallies the citizens of Paris to fight against Frollo. Phoebus is very loyal and would do anything for his friends. He catches Quasimodo when he falls off Notre Dame, saving his friend from plummeting to his death.

Frollo

Judge Claude Frollo has a twisted idea of justice. To validate his corrupt actions, he says they are God's will. Frollo attempts to get rid of Quasimodo as a baby and is stopped only by the interference of the Archdeacon. Tasked with caring for the baby, Frollo locks Quasimodo in a tower and refuses to let him join the outside world. Frollo hates the Romany people and believes that their "witchcraft" is blasphemous. He wants nothing more than to eliminate them from the city. The citizens of Paris are fearful of him, and Frollo commands an army of soldiers and thugs. He meets a fiery end when he tries to kill Esmeralda during his siege of Notre Dame: the gargoyle he stands on breaks off and roars at him before he plunges into a pool of lava below.

Mr. Incredible

Once the best-known, most popular Super alive, Bob Parr is now fifteen years older and sixty-four pounds heavier. As a claims adjuster at possibly the world's worst insurance company, Insuricare, the former Mr. Incredible's heroics are limited to helping people navigate the intricacies of the appeals system. More than anything, Bob wants to help people, but thanks to a series of lawsuits against Supers, he is not able to do so in the way he wants. Bob's unhappiness has taken a toll, and he and his family have become disconnected. Bob thinks the best years of his life are in the past until a new threat surfaces that only a Super can take on. Bob eagerly jumps into action, thrilled for the opportunity to use his powers again. When his wife is tasked with changing public perception about the Supers, Bob is forced to tackle fatherhood, alone. Eventually, Bob learns that the true source of power is his extraordinary family—and being a parent is truly a heroic act.

did you **know?**

- **Bob is six feet, seven inches tall and weighs 350 pounds.**

- **Bob first appeared on the cover of a comic book a boy was reading in the dentist's waiting room near the end of *Finding Nemo*, before making his official debut the next year.**

Elastigirl

Helen Parr, the former Elastigirl, has adjusted to normal life quite well and is focused on caring for her three children. While she occasionally uses her amazing ability to stretch to meet the daily challenges of modern motherhood, she is careful to do so only behind the closed doors of their suburban home. She misses the old days but doesn't dwell on those times, because she has a wonderful family and is quite happy to spend her time with them. But one day, Helen is offered the opportunity of a lifetime to bring Supers back into the spotlight. She is apprehensive about taking on hero work again at first, but she quickly proves to the public and herself that she can bring down the bad guys.

did you **know?**

- **Helen is in her late thirties. She is five feet, eight inches tall and weighs 125 pounds.**

- **As Elastigirl, Helen can make her body as thin as one millimeter. She can stretch her body up to three hundred feet and can leap up to eighty feet high.**

Violet

Violet Parr is in many ways a typically shy, insecure teenage girl. She, like her parents, has special powers, and it seems only right that hers allow her to turn invisible and protect herself with an equally invisible shield. What could be better for an awkward teen than to be able to disappear from her problems at a moment's notice—especially for someone who desperately wants to be normal like everyone else but truly isn't? Despite having a strong sibling rivalry with her brother Dash, Violet is fiercely protective of him. She is also starting to come into her own and master her Super powers of invisibility and force fields.

Dash

At age ten, Dash seems to be moving even when standing still. Full of restless energy, he has the power of Super speed—a power so useful for playing pranks that he has difficulty keeping it in check. Unable to resist torturing his least-favorite teacher, Dash has been called into the principal's office more than once, but he's never been caught. Dash doesn't understand why Supers should hide their powers. Why have them if they aren't supposed to use them?

Jack-Jack

Jack-Jack is the odd man out in the Parr family—or is he? Although the only incredible thing he seems to be able to do is jabber in gibberish, he is actually a polymorph with an array of hidden powers. These powers are on full display when he takes on an intruding raccoon in the Parrs' backyard. Despite his many powers, Jack-Jack is a typical baby who makes mealtime messes and insists on having a full bottle and clean diaper, especially during story time with his dad.

Frozone

Lucius Best used to be known as the coolest Super on the planet—and not just because he was best friends with Mr. Incredible. His style, wit, and attitude made Frozone, as he was known then, the hippest Super of the lot. Of course his powers made him cool, too—literally. Lucius's ability to create ice from moisture in the air and then travel on it with his special boots made him the envy of every gadget-loving little boy. Lucius knows the old days are done and there's no going back, so he doesn't try to relive the past. But he knows Bob still wants to, and he tries to help his friend adjust any way he can.

Syndrome

As a young and unusually zealous fan, Buddy vowed that one day he would become Mr. Incredible's sidekick, Incrediboy. But when he was told Mr. Incredible didn't want a sidekick, Buddy was torn apart. As Buddy grew older and bitterer, he got another idea: to be a Super, all you needed to do was save the world, right? So Buddy, now Syndrome, began to build and test the Omnidroid, a learning robotic weapon. Soon he'd be ready to let his invention wreak havoc on the world, so he could "save" it himself and at last become what he'd always wanted to be: a Super. Buddy is a classic sociopath. He doesn't care about the rules of society or who gets hurt in pursuit of his quest. He wants recognition for his greatness and will go to any lengths to get it.

did you **know?**

- **Syndrome's real name is Buddy Pine.**
- **Syndrome is in his mid-twenties. He is six feet, one inch tall and weighs 185 pounds.**

Edna Mode

Brilliant and successful, Edna got her start in the industry as the world's leading costume designer for Supers. With her now-mature sense of design, she remains the top designer in the field, taking her clothing designs to Milan, Paris, and other important international fashion centers. However, Edna longs for the return of the Supers, for a real design challenge, so she can fuse the latest technology with her impeccable fashion sense and unfurl her incredible creations for the adoring public. When Bob and the baby pay a visit to Edna's house, Edna gets very excited to create a new Supersuit for baby Jack-Jack.

did you **know?**

- **Edna is actually voiced by a man, *The Incredibles* writer-director Brad Bird.**

- **Edna's nickname is E.**

- **Edna is half Japanese and half German. Her last name literally translates to "fashion" in German.**

Mirage

Mirage is Syndrome's right-hand woman. Although she has no Super abilities herself, she does possess incredible skills with a computer. She even goes so far as to tell Mr. Incredible that, as far as the government is concerned, she does not exist. Mirage is a mysterious woman. She strings Mr. Incredible along, keeping her true purpose a secret. Although initially on board with Syndrome's plan, she changes her mind when she learns that Syndrome does not care if she lives or dies. Mirage realizes where her loyalties should truly lie and sets Mr. Incredible free to save his family and the world.

Gilbert Huph

Gilbert is Bob's boss at Insuricare. His top priority is making money for his company, and he doesn't care who gets hurt along the way. Gilbert is a stickler for bureaucracy and prefers that his customers not learn about any loopholes that might help them claim insurance money. Bob has trouble with Gilbert's philosophy and ultimately ends up in a fight with his boss that reveals his Super powers and gets him fired.

Winston Deavor

Winston is a mega-wealthy businessman, running a telecommunications company with his sister, Evelyn. Winston has been a huge supporter of the Supers ever since he lost his parents to a robbery gone awry when the Supers were forced into hiding. He needs Elastigirl's help to try to sway public opinion and bring the Supers back out of hiding.

Evelyn Deavor

Evelyn is Winston's sister and helps him run his telecommunications company. She loves tinkering with tech—especially optics—and may be hiding a secret or two.

The Screenslaver

Supervillain "The Screenslaver" devises high-powered public events for Elastigirl to solve, which boosts her popularity. The Screenslaver projects hypnotic light patterns onto screens of every type to hypnotize and take control of victims.

Tony Rydinger

A classmate and potential boyfriend of Violet's, he undergoes a memory wipe after seeing Violet in her Supersuit without her mask. Now poor Tony has no memory of the event, or of his upcoming date with Violet—in fact, he doesn't even remember who she is!

Riley Andersen

Riley is a cheerful eleven-year-old girl with a spirited imagination. She has a quiet confidence and is charmingly awkward. Whether she's building forts out of couch cushions, making bath time into a mermaid wonderland, or sliding down railings, Riley is able to turn ordinary experiences into extraordinary adventures. But her confidence is shaken when her family moves from Minnesota to San Francisco. Struggling to adjust to a new city and make new friends, Riley's happy-go-lucky personality starts to fade.

did you **know?**

- **Riley appears to be ambidextrous. She is shown as a toddler drawing Bing Bong on the walls with her left hand. She uses her right hand when she is eating.**

Mom

Jill Andersen prides herself on keeping her family stable and in check. With her boundless enthusiasm, she always finds the time to cheer at her daughter's ice hockey games. Though she is an unwavering supporter of her husband's new business venture, the move to San Francisco has proven to be even more work than this tireless mom expected.

Dad

Bill Andersen is a midwestern guy who's finally able to fulfill a lifelong dream of building his own startup in San Francisco. He's always been a caring, involved, and goofy father to his only daughter, Riley, but the new business requires a lot of attention. At his core, he's a good guy . . . a lover of sports who is terrifically bad at playing them, and a devoted husband who listens upward of 30 percent of the time.

Joy

Joy loves Riley more than anything and has been the little girl's lead Emotion since day one. She's lighthearted—a big fan of laughter, chocolate cake, and spinning until you get crazy dizzy and fall over. She sees life's challenges as opportunities and the sad bits as hiccups on the way back to something great. Hope and optimism dictate all her decisions, and Joy works twice as hard as anyone else to make that happen. She just wants Riley to be happy. After all, isn't that the point of life?

did you **know?**

- **Joy is the only Emotion whose hair and eye color is not the same as her theme color.**

- **During the development of the film, the Emotions were all going to have human names. Over time, the other Emotions' names changed, leaving Joy as the only one with a name also used by humans.**

- **Joy emits four light beams of different colors: blue, purple, white, and gold. The other Emotions each emit only one color.**

- **Joy's favorite Island of Personality is Goofball Island.**

Disgust

Disgust has always been proud of her refined tastes. For over a decade, her expert judgment has protected Riley from gross broccoli and helped her avoid icky boys. After all, her job is to keep Riley from being poisoned, physically or socially. Although highly opinionated and extremely honest, Disgust always has the best intentions. Her colleagues view her as a bit of an elitist, but Disgust refuses to lower her (and Riley's) standards for anybody. The world is a disgusting place, and it's her responsibility to say so.

Fear

There are very few things in life that Fear has not found to be dangerous and possibly fatal, including (but not limited to) roller skates, puppies, rain, and that strange noise coming from the basement some nights. Fear is always on the lookout for potential disasters ahead. He's keeping especially busy now that middle school has unveiled a fresh slate of perils. He does his best to protect Riley and keep her safe—no thanks to the other Emotions.

Sadness

Sadness has always been a "glass-half-empty" kind of Emotion. She'd love to be more optimistic, but it's hard to stay positive when the world's so full of misery. In just ten years, she's seen the deaths of Riley's three pet goldfish and the loss of a beloved purple troll doll. She's seen ice cream scoops fall to the ground for no reason and sand castles spontaneously cave in. Sometimes, Riley's life becomes so droopy, she has no choice but to collapse into a puddle of sorrow, "turn on the waterworks," and signal Mom and Dad for help. It's a painful job, but Sadness perseveres, one agonizing day at a time.

did you **know?**

- **Sadness's appearance is based on a teardrop.**

- **Even though Sadness is mostly seen as mournful, there are several occasions when she is seen smiling, proving that Emotions can express feelings other than the ones they represent.**

Anger

Anger tries to keep his cool, but it's difficult when there's so much rampant injustice in the world. He is quick to overreact, which results in rash decision-making and rude remarks. Ever since Riley turned two, Anger has been fighting the good fight, organizing tantrums for important causes such as "car seat liberation," "nap eradication," and "more cookies." It's a tough job, but someone's got to do it. Anger's impatience and impulsiveness ensure that all is fair in Riley's life.

Bing Bong

Bing Bong is Riley's imaginary friend. Unfortunately, he's been out of work since Riley turned four. He's a fun-loving, exuberant cat/elephant/dolphin made out of cotton candy wrapped around a nougat center. When Bing Bong is sad, he cries candy! Though Riley hasn't conjured up Bing Bong in years, he isn't giving up. His goal is to "get back in with Riley" so they can continue their imaginary games, like taking his song-powered rocket wagon to the moon.

Jangles the Clown

Riley was introduced to the ginormous Jangles the Clown at her cousin's birthday party when she was three. She was not amused . . . but he certainly made a huge impression and is now a permanent— and terrifying—fixture in Riley's Subconscious.

The Forgetters

The Forgetters (Paula and Bobby) are Mind Workers who select faded/unimportant memory spheres that are shelved in Long Term Memory to send down to the Memory Dump. Anything not worth remembering gets sucked into an enormous vacuum. By doing this, they make space on the shelves for new memory spheres. Goodbye, piano lessons! The Forgetters have a great sense of humor. Sometimes they like to play tricks on Riley and randomly send a memory (like the catchy Tripledent chewing gum commercial jingle) up to Headquarters.

Mowgli

Mowgli is a human boy who lives in the jungle. As a baby, he was discovered by the panther Bagheera and brought to live with a wolf pack. Mowgli has lived in the jungle for ten years. Although he knows he is not a wolf, Mowgli sees the wolves as his family and would happily stay with them for the rest of his life. But when the tiger Shere Khan returns to the jungle and threatens to kill the Man-cub, the wolves know it is time for Mowgli to go to the Man-village. Mowgli is fearless and often fails to recognize the dangers that lie in front of him. He is sure the tiger cannot hurt him and is determined to prove he can survive in the jungle, even if he must do so on his own. He is also stubborn, reckless, and impulsive. Mowgli acts without thinking, which frequently lands him in dangerous situations from which he must be saved.

did you **know?**

- **The animation of Mowgli was later used as inspiration when animating Aladdin.**

- **Mowgli makes a cameo at the end of *The Lion King 1½* and can be seen on a poster in *Meet the Robinsons*.**

Bagheera

Bagheera is a black panther. He is well-known to all the inhabitants of the jungle and is seemingly free to travel between the various herds of animals. It is Bagheera who finds Mowgli as a baby and brings him to the wolves. As Mowgli's rescuer, Bagheera feels a strong responsibility to the Man-cub. But Bagheera often loses his patience with Mowgli. He believes that he knows what is best for the boy, and does not take well to Mowgli believing otherwise. He similarly tends to lose his patience with the bear Baloo, whom he considers to be a fool. In spite of his occasional outbursts of temper, Bagheera is generally levelheaded. He prefers to come up with a plan rather than diving into action and faces dangerous situations with a calmness that allows him to think his way out of the situation.

did you **know?**

- **In the Russian version of the film, Bagheera is female. That is because the Russian word for "panther" is a feminine word.**

- **Bagheera means "black tiger" in Hindi.**

- **Although it is Bagheera's job to protect Mowgli from Shere Khan, the panther and the tiger never actually cross paths.**

Akela

Akela is the leader of the wolf pack. Strong and wise, it is he whom the other wolves listen to—even when they don't want to hear what he has to say. Akela welcomes Mowgli as part of the pack, and ultimately determines when it is time for him to leave. Despite his actions in dismissing Mowgli from the wolf pack, Akela is not without compassion. He just wants what is best for the majority of the pack.

Raksha

Raksha is Mowgli's adoptive mother. Warm and welcoming, she happily accepts Mowgli into her family and raises him as one of her own. Raksha's mate is Rama. Raksha is also mother to three young wolf cubs. Raksha does not speak. In spite of this, she can be quite persuasive, as seen when she silently convinces Rama to take in the orphaned Man-cub.

213

Baloo

Fun-loving and carefree, Baloo lives life to the fullest. He is not interested in taking on any responsibility, preferring to spend his days eating bananas and floating on the river. In fact, his life motto is to forget about worries and strife. Baloo tends to be a bit lazy, but he would do anything for his friends. The big bear has a heart of gold. He takes Mowgli under his wing, showing the Man-cub his own way of living in the jungle, and grows incredibly fond of the boy. He rescues Mowgli from the monkeys and even puts his own life on the line to protect Mowgli from the tiger Shere Khan. Although Baloo and Bagheera approach life completely differently, the two grow to be friends and ultimately work together to safely deliver Mowgli from the jungle.

did you **know?**

- **Baloo's trademark song, "The Bare Necessities," was the only song kept from the original draft of the film.**

- **Baloo stars in *TaleSpin*, a spin-off animated series. In the world of *TaleSpin*, Baloo is a skilled but lazy cargo pilot who struggles to pay his bills but always has time for his friends.**

Colonel Hathi

Colonel Hathi is the leader of the elephant herd. It is his responsibility to lead the Dawn Patrol, a job he takes very seriously. Colonel Hathi insists that all his elephants fall in line and allows no talking while in ranks. Hathi displays a particular distaste for Man, possibly as a result of having fought for humans before being released into the wild, and he grows quite angry upon learning that Mowgli has tried to join his platoon. Among Hathi's herd are his mate, Winifred, and his son.

The Baby Elephant

Hathi's son is a friendly little elephant. He happily invites Mowgli to join the Dawn Patrol's ranks, although he warns him not to speak. As Colonel Hathi's son, the little elephant has a wide knowledge of military terms. He looks up to his father and wants to be just like him. However, he is not quite as focused as his father. He is rather clumsy, and has a tendency to get lost and left behind by the rest of the Dawn Patrol. He is the youngest member of the herd and the only calf.

Shere Khan

Shere Khan is by far the most feared animal for miles around. More than anything, this vicious tiger hates Man. He is afraid of their fire and guns, and is willing to do anything to keep Man out of his home. Although the sight of fire drives Shere Khan into a state of panic, the ruthless tiger is generally calm and collected. He speaks with a manner of authority and expects others to do his bidding. He can easily intimidate Kaa, who is rightly feared by the other jungle animals. Shere Khan enlists the python to be his eyes and ears in the jungle as he searches for Mowgli, whom the tiger has made it his mission to kill.

did you **know?**

- **Shere Khan's name means "Tiger King" in Persian and Hindi.**

- **Shere Khan is immune to Kaa's hypnosis skills.**

- **The animation that was created for Shere Khan was later used as reference for the characters in _The Lion King_.**

King Louie

King Louie is the king of the apes. He kidnaps Mowgli so that the Man-cub can teach him the secret of "Man's red flower"— fire! This royal orangutan leads a lavish life. He resides in an abandoned temple and seems to have an endless supply of bananas. He is somewhat laid-back, loving little more than a good party, but he is also incredibly cunning. Louie knows how to keep his minions in line, and he recognizes that Mowgli's naive nature makes the Man-cub easy to manipulate. King Louie feels that he has reached the limit of what he can achieve in the jungle, and this frustrates him. He wants to learn the secret of fire so that he can become like Man and go on to bigger, better things.

Kaa

Kaa is one of the most dangerous creatures in the jungle. The sly python speaks in a soft, lulling voice to calm his victims and then hypnotizes them with his eyes and squeezes them tightly in his coils. Kaa inspires fear in most of the other jungle animals, who go out of their way to avoid him. Kaa is not generally picky about who he chooses as his prey, but he does not take kindly to his food getting away and has been shown to hold a grudge. In spite of his fearsome nature, Kaa tends to be rather humorously clumsy. He is also easily distracted, especially by Mowgli.

Lady

Lady is exactly what her name implies: a lady inside and out. Raised in the lap of luxury, Lady is thoroughly faithful to her adoring humans, Jim Dear and Darling, and knows little of the hostile world a dog on the streets can face. But when her owners go on vacation, she's muzzled by Aunt Sarah and runs away, only to be cornered by a pack of wild street dogs. Out of nowhere, Tramp leaps to her defense. The independent charmer shows Lady that while there's danger in the outside world, there's also life: a world of adventure where beavers can be conned into removing muzzles and a dark alley can become the site of a romantic dinner. For all Lady's sweetness, she has a colder side, too. She can hold a grudge, and she does when she thinks Tramp has wronged her. But she is also able to forgive. In the end, Lady can't help herself. She falls head over heels for the charming mutt.

did you **know?**

- **Lady was inspired by a drawing one of Walt Disney's "storymen" showed him of his own cocker spaniel.**

- **In an early version of the script, it was Lady who was meant to kill the rat in the baby's bedroom.**

- **Tramp's pet name for Lady is Pidge.**

Jim Dear

A young middle-class couple, Jim Dear and Darling are delightful pet owners. Jim Dear is a businessman who wears a sober brown three-piece suit and matching bowler hat and has a small, well-groomed mustache. He has a great sense of fun and play, as he demonstrates each evening when Lady greets him. Jim seems to understand Lady well. He knows when she wants him to follow her and understands when she is trying to tell him that something is wrong. His true name is not Jim Dear. Rather, this is the name Darling calls him, and as such, the only name known to Lady.

Darling

Darling has pretty brown hair and dresses modestly. She knits and sews and keeps the house in order, looking after her husband dutifully. Darling is also the proud mother of a bouncing baby boy and the loving owner of Lady. It was to Darling whom Lady was given one Christmas morning by Jim Dear. Lady does not know Darling's real name. She has only ever heard Jim Dear call his wife Darling, so she thinks of that as her mistress's name.

Tramp

Footloose and collar-free, Tramp lives every day as if it were his last. Although he's just one step ahead of the dogcatcher, Tramp is too busy playing with danger to be scared of it. He's that rare breed of dog who wants no master but himself. Living by his wits, he's learned that if you have a little charm and a lot of finesse, the world can be your dinner bowl. Tramp has a different home—with a different type of cuisine—for every night of the week. The irresistible rogue does have one weakness: the ladies. Indeed, Tramp falls in love with the winsome Lady and finds himself willing to risk life and limb more than once for her. He also finds that living in a home isn't as bad as he previously believed.

did you **know?**

- **Early versions of the script had Tramp's name as Homer, Hobo, Rags, and Bozo.**

Jock

Jock is the epitome of the Scottish terrier in every sense, from his stubby physique to his slightly gruff personality, which is tempered by his essential good nature. He's the one who discourages Trusty from repeating tales of his grandfather Old Reliable, but he also conceals from the unfortunate bloodhound the painful fact that Trusty has lost his sense of smell. Although Jock is not fond of Tramp, he does his best to save his life. He also learns to trust the street dog once he is taken into the Darling household, and he grows to be quite fond of Lady and Tramp's four pups.

Trusty

This poor old bloodhound has lost his sense of smell, but nobody has the heart to tell him. In the old days, he and his grandfather Old Reliable used to stalk criminals all over the world. Trusty is fond of telling tales about his grandfather, although he can never quite seem to recall how they end. Trusty is incredibly fond of Lady and feels very protective of her. He is more trusting than Jock and does not display as strong a dislike for Tramp. It is he who saves Tramp from the dogcatcher, although he gets injured in the process. Trusty is proud to be an uncle to Lady and Tramp's four pups.

Peg

Peg the dog is a musical stray with a motherly, comforting personality. She is one of the dogs Lady meets during her time in the pound. Peg knows Tramp well and sings to Lady about his charisma. She even admits that she has a little crush on him! Peg has fluffy, shaggy fur that flops in front of her blue eyes. She also has all-natural violet "eye shadow."

The Beaver

A beaver with teeth like steel, this busy critter doesn't have time for gossip! Although distrustful of Lady and Tramp at first, the beaver soon warms up to Lady and helps remove her muzzle. This guy is incredibly resourceful: he uses his tail as a measuring tool, and when Tramp suggests it, he sees how the muzzle can be used as a log carrier.

Si and Am

Si and Am, twin Siamese cats, prowl in harmony and wreak havoc all around them. Cunning and spiteful, they display the worst traits of their species. As they vandalize Jim Dear and Darling's home, terrorizing the pet goldfish and canary, Lady is helpless to stop the chaos. When they proceed upstairs to steal the baby's milk, Lady takes the offensive, barring their way with a fearsome growl. But, too devious for the innocent Lady, they end up framing her for all their destruction. As much their patsy as Lady herself, Aunt Sarah carries them off, exclaiming, "Oh, that wicked animal—attacking my poor, innocent little angels."

Aunt Sarah

Though matronly Aunt Sarah is a pushover for cats, she just won't give a dog an even break. When she takes over the household to babysit in Jim Dear and Darling's absence, she keeps Lady from the nursery. When the baby cries, Lady gets the blame. Soon after, Aunt Sarah's coddled Siamese cats secretly demolish the living room, and again, she blames the dog. Not unlike a cat, Aunt Sarah is obstinate, self-centered, and set in her ways. Indeed, her answer to the "Lady problem" is to have the poor dog muzzled. But as can happen with such narrow-minded types, her own misconceptions finally lead to her undoing. Lady's muzzling touches off a course of events that leaves the baby unprotected when he needs Lady the most.

Scamp

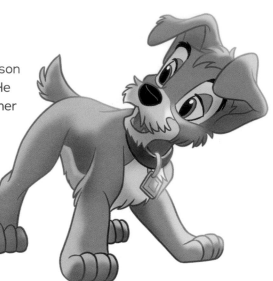

Scamp is the rascally son of Lady and Tramp. He looks just like his father and has the same sense of adventure. Scamp loves to explore and often finds himself in trouble, but Scamp doesn't mind. For him, getting in trouble is all part of the fun!

Annette, Colette, and Danielle

Scamp's three siblings, Annette, Colette, and Danielle, look just like their mother. The three act like her as well. They generally follow the rules and do as they are told, but that doesn't mean they don't like to play. These three can get in their fair share of trouble, too—they just tend to feel worse about it.

Joe

The chef at Tony's Restaurant is about half the size of Tony, but equally big in spirit and personality. Dressed in a full chef's outfit, he, too, has a black mustache. His eyes sparkle as he plays the mandolin during Tony's rendition of "Bella Notte." He can sense love in the air and is pleased to be able to play his part in making it bloom.

Lilo

Something about Lilo makes you want to hug her. She's a cheerful, adorable, die-hard Elvis fan and a passionate aficionado of all things bizarre. Her vivid imagination is one of her greatest gifts . . . and sometimes the cause of her biggest problems. It's not always easy being the most unique person on her island, especially when her quirkiness keeps her from making friends. Although Lilo seems fiercely independent for a six-year-old, she is also extremely vulnerable, especially regarding the issues of loneliness and abandonment. Ever since the death of her parents, everyone has been treating Lilo differently, and she knows it. The only thing she wants more than staying with her sister, Nani, is finding a friend who won't leave her. Lilo finds more than she ever could have hoped for in Stitch, a creature who also just wants to be loved.

did you **know?**

- **Lilo's name can mean both "lost" and "the generous one" in Hawaiian.**
- **Lilo enjoys feeding peanut butter sandwiches to her fish, Pudge.**

Nani

Nani is Lilo's older sister. After the death of their parents, Nani became Lilo's legal guardian, which is a lot of responsibility for a young woman who used to enjoy carefree days of dating and surf championships. Now life is a pressure cooker of daily challenges as Nani tries to hold down a job, raise a small child, and elude the constant scrutiny of the Child Welfare Department so she can maintain custody of her little sister. The most important thing to Nani is keeping what is left of her family together.

David

David is a strapping, tanned twenty-three-year-old Hawaiian surfer. Those who might assume he's just another addled, dim-witted "surf dude" will find themselves mistaken. Behind his calm demeanor, David is quite intelligent, with a quick wit and slightly odd sense of humor. David and Nani used to date, but the pressures of raising Lilo have forced them to be just "good friends." David earns his living as the fire dancer at the hotel where Nani works as a waitress. He has been known to burn himself, as well as parts of the restaurant, while throwing his torches around.

Stitch

Stitch is the only creature of his kind in existence. He is the result of an illegal genetic experiment by the mad scientist Jumba Jukiba, who simply refers to his creation as Experiment 626. Although Stitch appears harmless, his very existence is an abomination to all that's decent in the galaxy. Jumba engineered Stitch as the ultimate fighting machine: abnormally strong, virtually indestructible, and smarter than a supercomputer. Stitch cannot control his preprogrammed urge to destroy until he finds the one thing he has never known before: a family. Stitch is capable of speaking only a few words. Still, his big black eyes and droopy ears are very expressive and allow him to convey his feelings. He risks everything to show Nani that not only can he speak, but he loves Lilo and will risk his life for her.

did you **know?**

- **Stitch's body is incredibly dense, making it impossible for him to swim or float.**

- **Stitch's favorite book is *The Ugly Duckling*.**

- **Stitch was not originally supposed to talk, but when the filmmakers realized the story hinged on his being able to express himself at the film's end, they began developing his voice.**

Cobra Bubbles

Cobra Bubbles is the ultimate social worker. He is a no-nonsense, cunning, unshakable master of the art of child welfare. Nani and Lilo have already worn out quite a few other social workers, so the system has sent in "the big guns." Despite his professional demeanor, Cobra soon finds himself both baffled and charmed by Lilo's quirky personality. He struggles to remain impartial as his affection for the two sisters grows. Cobra's methods may seem harsh, but he truly wants what is best for Lilo, even if it isn't staying with Nani.

did you **know?**

- **Prior to becoming a social worker, Cobra Bubbles worked for the CIA.**

- **Cobra Bubbles knows the Grand Councilwoman who wants Stitch captured from his previous work. They crossed paths in Roswell.**

Jumba

A renegade scientist, Jumba Jukiba was imprisoned due to unlawful experiments that resulted in the creation of the genetic mutation Experiment 626 (later named Stitch). Brilliant but overzealous, Jumba is eager to regain his freedom by traveling to Earth to capture Stitch. His large frame, multiple eyes, and thick Russian accent make him an unlikely candidate for the undercover mission, but his expertise cannot be denied: he knows Stitch better than anyone else in the universe, because he created him.

Pleakley

An enthusiastic Earth hobbyist, Pleakley is uptight, nervous, and rule-bound. He is the only alien with any knowledge of the distant planet Earth. The Grand Councilwoman puts Pleakley in charge of a covert mission to retrieve Stitch and pairs him with Jumba. Unfortunately, all Pleakley's knowledge of Earth comes from a GAF View-Master, so his expertise on the planet and its inhabitants is somewhat skewed, to say the least. Pleakley can be a bit obnoxious, accentuated by his high-pitched voice, his know-it-all attitude (especially regarding Earth), and his tendency to panic at inappropriate times. He also has a very strong moral compass and is driven by his sense of right and wrong.

Simba

As heir to King Mufasa's throne, Simba has been taught to respect all creatures, great and small. They are all part of the Circle of Life. Simba is curious about the world around him and eager to explore. He is mischievous and generally acts fearless—unless placed in actual danger. He is also rather arrogant, thinking himself above Mufasa's majordomo, Zazu, since he will one day be the bird's king. When Simba's uncle Scar initiates a wildebeest stampede that kills Mufasa, he blames the cub for his father's death and convinces him to run away. Cast out into exile, Simba must fend for himself. With the help of Timon and Pumbaa, he chooses a lifestyle of *hakuna matata*: no responsibilities, no cares. Simba is desperate to forget his past, but when his old friend Nala appears, pleading with him to save the Pride Lands from Scar, Simba springs into action to take his rightful place in the Circle of Life as the Lion King.

did you **know?**

- **Simba means "lion" in Swahili.**
- **Early concept art of Simba shows him with blue eyes.**

Mufasa

Mufasa is a stern but kind leader. Courageous yet cautious, Mufasa is feared by the hyenas and respected by everyone except for his brother, Scar. Mufasa's jealous brother is a thorn in the king's side, but Mufasa still looks out for him, hoping that someday he will change. He is also a caring and nurturing father and adoring husband. He has high aspirations—and high expectations—for his son, Simba, the heir to his throne. Mufasa hopes that his son will be a wise leader, and teaches him the true meaning of bravery. Mufasa would do anything for his son, and he does, ultimately losing his life in an attempt to rescue Simba.

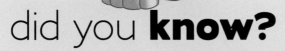

did you **know?**

- **The name Mufasa means "king" in the Manazoto language.**

- **In an early script for *The Lion King*, Mufasa sang a song called "Mighty King of the Wild." It was cut since it didn't match Mufasa's character.**

Nala

Sweet, adorable Nala is Simba's best friend and companion. She would do anything for the future king. Like Simba, she is curious about the world around her and loves to explore. Nala pretends to be fearless and can always beat Simba in a fight. It is Nala who finds her long-lost friend and convinces him to return to the Pride Lands and overthrow Scar. When Simba finally takes the throne, Nala becomes his bride and queen of the Pride Lands.

Sarabi

Behind every strong lion king, there's a strong lioness. Queen Sarabi is a regal, caring mother and wife. Loyal and brave, she's not afraid to stand up to the evil Scar. She tries to convince the new king, who takes over the Pride Lands when Mufasa dies, that they all must leave Pride Rock because there is no food left. She cares enough about the welfare of the other animals in the kingdom to risk provoking the mean-spirited Scar.

Timon

Timon is a wisecracking meerkat who leads the *hakuna matata* lifestyle of no worries, no responsibilities, and no cares. Timon realizes that having a lion on his side will keep him protected from other predators, so he and Pumbaa take Simba in and raise him. But, of course, it's hard to have *no* worries, and when Nala shows up, Timon fears Simba will leave him and Pumbaa behind. When he realizes this fear is coming true, he sets out to help his friend and plays a role in saving the Pride Lands and restoring Simba to his throne.

Pumbaa

Pumbaa is a warthog with a bit of a gas problem. He is the brains of his group, although he doesn't realize it, as Timon has a tendency to take credit for Pumbaa's bright ideas. Pumbaa has a big heart and would do anything for his friends— even share his grubs. When Simba is called into action to save the Pride Lands, Pumbaa and Timon discover that they are warriors at heart (even if they are silly ones).

Rafiki

Rafiki is a wise baboon and a shaman. He's somewhat mysterious and a little crazy. It is Rafiki's job to present new lion cubs to the rest of the kingdom, and he never forgets a face. Rafiki helps Simba come to terms with who he is and embrace his place in the Circle of Life.

Zazu

A hornbill, Zazu is Mufasa's majordomo. He takes his job very seriously. He's also a worrier. Much to his dismay, he is often put in the position of being Simba's babysitter—a difficult task, since Simba wants nothing more than to run away from him. Zazu puts up with a lot of teasing from Simba but still watches out for the rambunctious young lion. Zazu lives life by the rules, and he expects others to do the same. This frequently puts him at odds with Scar, who imprisons the bird once he takes over the Pride Lands.

Scar

Scar, the evil brother of King Mufasa and second in line to the throne, wants to be king. Scar is a close companion of the hyenas who live in the Elephant Graveyard. They take his orders, and in return he makes sure they have plenty of food. He is an out-and-out villain: witty, slimy, seductive, and willing to do anything to gain power—even if it means killing his brother in a wildebeest stampede. Scar convinces Simba that he was responsible for his father's death and then gleefully takes over the throne. As bad guys are inclined to do, Scar lets the Pride Lands slip into desperate trouble. It is to a destroyed Pride Rock that Simba returns to do battle with his uncle. Although strong and conniving, Scar cannot overcome the sheer anger Simba feels at learning the truth about his father's death. The two battle and Scar loses, doomed by his own betrayals.

did you **know?**

• **Scar hates the song "It's a Small World."**

Shenzi, Banzai, and Ed

The hyenas are outcasts among the other animals and make their home in the Elephant Graveyard, a place outside the boundaries of the Pride Lands. Shenzi, Banzai, and Ed are Scar's henchmen. They do his bidding and help him rid the Pride Lands of Mufasa and Simba. In return, they are given full run of the Pride Lands. Shenzi is the leader of the hyenas and the only female in Scar's trio of minions. She is calm and collected, rarely losing her temper. The other hyenas listen to her without question. Shenzi is wise enough to put aside her dislike of Scar in favor of finding a better situation for herself and her friends. Banzai, on the other hand, is all aggression. He loves a good fight and thinks with his stomach rather than his head. Ed is the true comic relief of the group. His eyes seem unable to focus, his tongue lolls out of his mouth, and he laughs at everything—even things that aren't funny.

Ariel

The youngest daughter of King Triton, Ariel loves music, exploring, and above all, the human world. Ariel is fiercely independent. Despite her father's orders never to go to the surface of the ocean, the little mermaid can't help herself. She is fascinated by the human world and longs to be a part of it. She even collects human treasures from sunken ships. Ariel's life is turned on its ear when she rescues a human prince named Eric from a shipwreck and falls in love with him. Desperate after a fight with her father, Ariel makes a deal with the sea witch, Ursula, and trades her voice for the chance to be human for three days. Although things do not go to plan, Eric does fall in love with Ariel and—with the help of King Triton—the two are married. Although Ariel now lives on land with Prince Eric and their dog, Max, she still loves the sea and visits her friends and family often.

did you **know?**

- **The blue-green hue of Ariel's tail was specially mixed by the Disney paint lab. They called the new color "Ariel" in her honor.**

- **The iconic pose of Ariel sitting on a rock watching Eric was inspired by the famous *The Little Mermaid* statue in Copenhagen, Denmark.**

Flounder

Flounder is Ariel's best and most loyal friend. He loves to explore the depths of the ocean with her and collect human treasures. Like Ariel, Flounder is fascinated by human objects and longs to know what they do. Flounder is easily frightened, but he is also capable of great bravery—as long as the source of the danger he fears isn't too close! Flounder loves Ariel and would follow her anywhere, including to the surface. In fact, he helps her reach land when she trades her voice for legs. Flounder may be little, but he has a big heart!

did you **know?**

- **Flounder makes a cameo in *Moana*. He can be seen among the tapa cloth fish during the song "You're Welcome."**

- **Ariel refers to Flounder as a guppy, but he is actually an unspecified type of tropical fish.**

- **In an early draft of the script, Ariel's best friend was a dolphin named Breaker. This character was later replaced by Flounder.**

Sebastian

Sebastian is the court composer and one of King Triton's most trusted advisers. In fact, Triton gives Sebastian the job of keeping an eye on Ariel, a task the little crab takes quite seriously. Although Sebastian respects King Triton greatly, he also fears him, often worrying about what the king will do to him if he makes a mistake. Sebastian is highly intelligent and practical. Like King Triton, he dislikes the surface world. But for Sebastian, this dislike comes largely from a fear of being eaten! Despite his no-nonsense personality, Sebastian has a soft spot for Ariel. Although he often finds her short attention span and unwillingness to listen to her father frustrating, he takes it upon himself to help her once she becomes human and does his best to make Eric fall in love with her.

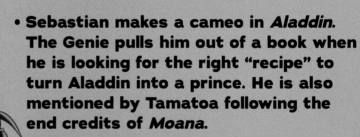

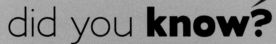

did you **know?**

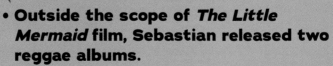

- **Sebastian makes a cameo in *Aladdin*. The Genie pulls him out of a book when he is looking for the right "recipe" to turn Aladdin into a prince. He is also mentioned by Tamatoa following the end credits of *Moana*.**

- **Outside the scope of *The Little Mermaid* film, Sebastian released two reggae albums.**

Ariel's Sisters

Ariel may be King Triton's most challenging daughter, but she's far from his only child. Ariel has six older sisters. Their names are Aquata, Andrina, Arista, Attina, Adella, and Alana. Although Ariel's sisters love her dearly, they don't understand her. They are perfectly happy with their lives under the sea and cannot fathom Ariel's fascination with the human world. Like Ariel, her sisters all have lovely voices. In fact, they are the singers in the choir conducted by Sebastian the crab.

King Triton

The mighty King Triton rules the seas and all of Atlantica with a firm hand— and a magical golden trident. Triton is not a fan of humans. In fact, he has forbidden his subjects to visit the surface or interact with humans in any way. Triton expects his rules to be followed and does not take kindly to being disobeyed. In spite of his sternness, Triton has a soft spot for his daughters. He is thrilled when he thinks Ariel has fallen in love with a merman and cannot wait to meet the lucky man. He also worries greatly and blames himself when Ariel falls into Ursula's clutches, even going so far as to sacrifice himself to save her. For all his harsh feelings toward the human world, Triton is not afraid to admit when he has made a mistake. Seeing Eric's love for Ariel, he admits that he may have judged the prince too quickly. In the end, it is he who transforms Ariel permanently into a human so that she can be with the man she loves.

Ursula

The half-octopus Ursula is an incredibly powerful sea witch. Luring "poor, unfortunate souls" to her home, Ursula happily creates potions and casts spells. But her intentions are not so pure, and she goes out of her way to make sure her customers fail to live up to their ends of the bargains they've made. Ursula was banished from Atlantica by King Triton long ago and has held a grudge against him ever since. She sees Ariel's love for Eric as her chance to get revenge and gain what she wants more than anything—power over the seas. Ursula easily convinces Ariel to make a deal with her. She then sets about making sure Ariel fails, even going so far as to disguise herself as a human named Vanessa to keep Eric from kissing Ariel. Although Ursula's plot succeeds and she manages not only to trade Ariel's soul for Triton's but to take over as queen of Atlantica, she is ultimately defeated and killed by Prince Eric.

did you **know?**

- **Ursula's octopus half has only six tentacles. The other two limbs are her arms!**

- **In an early draft of the film, Ursula was King Triton's sister, which would have made her Ariel's aunt.**

Scuttle

Scuttle lives on a small rock in the ocean, not far from Prince Eric's castle. This dim-witted seagull thinks he knows everything about the human world, although what he *actually* knows may be a little off base. Scuttle is incredibly fond of Ariel. He happily shares his knowledge with her and does his best to help her win the heart of Prince Eric. Scuttle has a tendency to get flustered and mix up his words when he is startled, but he always comes through in the end. It is he who discovers that the sea witch Ursula has disguised herself as a human to stop Ariel from winning over Eric.

Flotsam and Jetsam

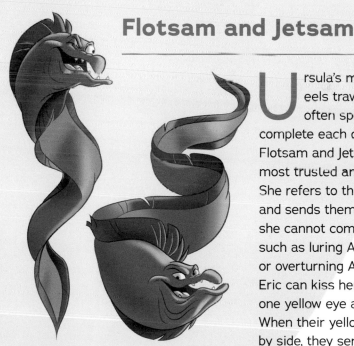

Ursula's minions, these two eels travel together and often speak in unison or complete each other's sentences. Flotsam and Jetsam are Ursula's most trusted and beloved spies. She refers to them as her babies and sends them out on missions she cannot complete herself, such as luring Ariel to her cave or overturning Ariel's boat before Eric can kiss her. Each eel has one yellow eye and one white eye. When their yellow eyes are side by side, they serve as a crystal ball, allowing Ursula to see what they see.

Prince Eric

Eric is a hopeless romantic. He believes in love at first sight—or rather, sound. He knows he loves the girl who saved him from the shipwreck; he just doesn't know what she looks like. But he'll never forget the sound of her voice. Eric's big heart extends beyond just romantic love. He is also incredibly fond of his manservant, Grimsby, and is a loyal owner to his dog, Max. Eric is an accomplished mariner and an excellent flute player. Although he understands the responsibility that comes with being a prince and the future king, he remains lighthearted. He enjoys having a good time and encourages those around him to do the same. Eric easily falls under Ursula's spell, but true love ultimately wins out. He realizes that Ariel is the girl he loves and the two are married.

did you **know?**

- **Eric has the first speaking line in *The Little Mermaid*.**

Max

Prince Eric's sheepdog, Max is a loyal part of the royal family. Playful and affectionate, Max takes an immediate liking to Ariel, whom he finds on the beach. But Max does not like just anyone. Upon meeting Vanessa, he begins to growl at her, clearly able to sense that she is not what she seems.

Grimsby

Grimsby is Prince Eric's manservant and confidant. Where Eric goes, so goes Grimsby—even aboard Eric's ship, despite the fact that Grimsby suffers from seasickness. Although stuffy and uptight, Grimsby cares deeply for Eric. He wishes to see him married and cannot understand why Eric is so picky about selecting a wife. Grimsby is realistic. He does not believe the myths about the great King Triton and dismisses Eric's claim of being saved by a beautiful girl as a delusion caused by the prince's having swallowed too much seawater.

Mike "Goob" Yagoobian

Goob is Lewis's roommate at the orphanage. Although he puts up with Lewis's constant inventing, the gadgets don't really interest him. He's much more interested in baseball. After Lewis keeps him up all night while inventing a Memory Scanner, Goob is so tired that he misses making the game-winning catch in his baseball game. For Goob, that's one step too far. He falls into a state of constant anger, which turns off potential adoptive parents. As a result, Goob is never adopted, and he holds Lewis solely responsible for that.

Bowler Hat Guy

An incredibly angry future version of Goob, Bowler Hat Guy dresses fully in black and considers himself a cunning, intimidating villain. For years, Bowler Hat Guy has nursed his anger about missing the game-winning catch in his Little League game and grown more and more furious with Lewis as he has heard of the inventor's successes. Eager to change the past, he steals a time machine. Unfortunately for Bowler Hat Guy, he's not nearly as clever as he thinks he is, and he is easily tricked by a robotic bowler hat named Doris. It is only with the help of Lewis that he is able to defeat Doris, set the past right, and finally find a way to resolve the events of that fateful spring day when he failed to catch the baseball.

Lewis

Lewis is a twelve-year-old boy with an incredibly high IQ and a talent for inventing things. He is also an orphan, which causes him unending dismay. More than anything, Lewis longs for a family of his own. Unfortunately, time and again, his offbeat nature and his unintentionally disastrous inventions sabotage his hopes of achieving that dream. Lewis was abandoned as an infant by his mother and has come to believe that she left because she could not care for him. Now that he is older, he hopes to change her mind. To that end, he builds a Memory Scanner to extract his only memory of her. Lewis wishes he could go back in time and change his life so he won't be an orphan, but instead he learns that he must accept his life as it is and keep moving forward.

did you **know?**

- **Lewis's hobby of creating bizarre inventions scares off 124 families looking to adopt.**

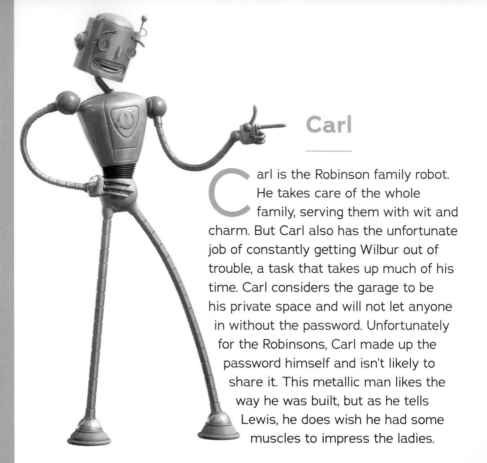

Carl

Carl is the Robinson family robot. He takes care of the whole family, serving them with wit and charm. But Carl also has the unfortunate job of constantly getting Wilbur out of trouble, a task that takes up much of his time. Carl considers the garage to be his private space and will not let anyone in without the password. Unfortunately for the Robinsons, Carl made up the password himself and isn't likely to share it. This metallic man likes the way he was built, but as he tells Lewis, he does wish he had some muscles to impress the ladies.

Bud Robinson

Grandpa Bud may seem weird to the outside world, but to the Robinsons, he just views life a little differently. Bud likes to wear his clothes backward and has painted a smiley face on the back of his head. He is a bit forgetful. This funny fellow is always losing his teeth and asking for help finding them.

Wilbur Robinson

Wilbur Robinson is a mysterious boy from the future who claims to be a Time Continuum Task Force officer. In reality, Wilbur is Lewis's future son. Wilbur's greatest flaws—inflated self-confidence and a cocky attitude—are also his greatest assets. They allow Wilbur to stay one step ahead of his enemies. Although Wilbur knows who Lewis is, he is careful to keep the truth from Lewis. After all, the future rests on Lewis, and Wilbur is determined to set its course straight.

did you **know?**

- **Searching for a description of someone who looks the opposite of his father, Wilbur tells Lewis that his father looks like Tom Selleck. In reality, Tom Selleck is the voice actor who plays Wilbur's father.**

Doris

Doris, initially named Dor-15, was created as a helping hat that would assist wearers in achieving small tasks. But Doris had other ideas. Pure evil at heart, she wanted to rule humanity and took control of the test wearer. Her inventor, Cornelius Robinson, tried to deactivate her but failed. Doris teams up with Bowler Hat Guy, tricking him into thinking he is in charge. But when Bowler Hat Guy changes the future, Doris is obliterated, never having been invented in the first place.

Franny Robinson

Franny is the mother of Wilbur Robinson and the wife of Lewis Robinson. She is a caring and fun-loving mother and wife. She is extremely compassionate, as demonstrated when she offers to take Lewis in, knowing he has no family—and not suspecting that Lewis is Cornelius, her husband, from the past.

Mickey Mouse

This little guy started it all for Walt Disney when he became the star of a number of Walt's earliest cartoons. First created as a mischievous rascal, Mickey has transformed over the years into an all-around nice guy. Sometimes shy, sometimes brave, and sometimes silly, Mickey is a dog's best friend (to Pluto) and sweetheart to Minnie Mouse. He loves adventure and trying new things, although his plans tend to go awry more often than not. Mickey usually appears in his signature red shorts, yellow shoes, and white gloves.

did you **know?**

- **Mickey Mouse was almost named Mortimer.**

- **Mickey made his debut in *Steamboat Willie* on November 18, 1928 (which makes it his birthday)!**

- **Mickey was the first animated character to receive a star on the Hollywood Walk of Fame.**

Minnie Mouse

Minnie Mouse is nothing if not a fashion icon. Although she usually appears in her trademark red-and-white polka-dot dress and bow with yellow shoes, she has been seen in over two hundred different outfits! Minnie is incredibly sweet and good-hearted, though she has been known to lose her temper at times, especially at Mickey's forgetfulness. Minnie is also a hopeless romantic—a side she shows off when talking about longtime sweetheart Mickey—a fiercely loyal friend, and a wonderful pet owner to her little kitten, Figaro. Her best girl pal is Daisy Duck. The two friends love to spend time together, sharing ideas and going on adventures.

did you **know?**

- **Minnie's full name is Minerva.**
- **Minnie's catchphrase is "Yoo-hoo."**
- **Minnie's cat, Figaro, is the same cat who appears in *Pinocchio*.**
- **Minnie's parents are farmers.**
- **Minnie got her star on the Hollywood Walk of Fame in 2018.**

Pluto

Pluto is Mickey Mouse's ever-faithful pup. He is always very clear about his feelings. Friendly, loyal, and fiercely protective of Mickey, Pluto is also rather mischievous. When he gets into trouble, he "apologizes" by sheepishly putting his tail between his legs. Pluto also has a particular dislike for cats, especially Minnie's cat, Figaro. He's been known to chase Figaro, as well as Chip and Dale. But most of the time Pluto is a very good dog.

Morty and Ferdie Fieldmouse

Morty and Ferdie are the identical twin nephews of Mickey Mouse. Their mother is Mickey's older sister, Amely Mouse-Fieldmouse. The twins often come to stay with Mickey and even have their own room at his house. Each twin has his own interests. Morty is fascinated by how various devices and mechanisms work and likes building them on his own. Ferdie loves baseball and reading and can often be found listening to pop and rock music.

Donald Duck

Donald is one hot-tempered fella with a heart of gold. He always seems to be getting into some kind of trouble. Donald is quick to get angry and frustrated, but he is also brave, determined, and stubborn, and he would do anything for his family. He is lazy but inventive, and he always starts a new adventure with much optimism and enthusiasm. He's great pals with Mickey Mouse, and Daisy Duck will always be his sweetheart.

did you **know?**

- **Donald's middle name is Fauntleroy.**

- **Donald first appeared six years after Mickey Mouse.**

Clarabelle Cow

Clarabelle is one of Minnie Mouse's best friends. She is extremely kind and a good friend, although she can sometimes be rather clumsy. Unlike Mickey and his other friends, Clarabelle's animal nature tends to shine through. She often wears cowbells as jewelry and speaks in cow-related puns.

Pete

Pete is Mickey Mouse's nemesis and the primary villain of Mickey's world. Although often mistaken for a dog due to his large size, Pete is actually a cat. Pete comes from a long line of villains and outlaws. His mother, known only as "Maw Pete," is a criminal mastermind. Pete also has a sister named Petula and a longtime girlfriend named Trudy. Pete has gone by several names, including Peg-Leg Pete, Pistol Pete, and Big Bad Pete.

Daisy Duck

Daisy Duck is romantic, sophisticated, modern, and sometimes temperamental, especially when she has to deal with her sweetheart, Donald Duck. She is always looking for perfection. She loves shopping, having fun with her friends, and spending as much time as she can with her best friend, Minnie Mouse.

did you **know?**

- **Daisy was originally named Donna.**

- **Daisy was renamed in 1940. She made her first appearance as Daisy in the short *Mr. Duck Steps Out*.**

- **Daisy has three nieces: April, May, and June.**

Huey, Dewey, and Louie

Huey, Dewey, and Louie are Donald Duck's inventive and dynamic nephews. These three little guys have a great sense of adventure and fun. They have an unbreakable bond and do nearly everything together. Brave and clever, these identical triplets love their uncle and their family.

Grandma Duck

Grandma Duck is the grandmother of Donald Duck and the great-grandmother of Huey, Dewey, and Louie. She has three children: Quackmore (Donald's father), Daphne, and Eider. Grandma Duck is the matriarch of the Duck family. She hosts family gatherings at her farm and is often praised for her impressive cooking skills.

Scrooge McDuck

Scrooge McDuck is Donald's uncle. His sister Hortense is Donald's mother. Scrooge is a wealthy Scottish businessduck. In fact, he is the richest duck in all of Duckburg. Scrooge worked hard for every cent he has and he hates to part with any of it, no matter the cause. Scrooge keeps his money in his "money bin" and loves nothing more than diving in and swimming through his golden coins. Scrooge left school at an early age, but he is sharp-witted and always ready to learn new skills. In addition to running his business, he has a secondary career as a treasure hunter and is something of an amateur archaeologist.

Chip and Dale

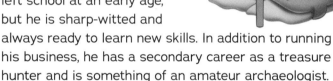

Chip and Dale are two little chipmunks with two big personalities. Chip is more responsible and no-nonsense, while Dale is a bit more scatterbrained and easygoing. They are always trying to gather a great stockpile of acorns . . . and if they can tease their friends Donald and Pluto in the process, all the better! Chip and Dale are the best of friends and are rarely seen apart from each other. Chip has a small black nose (like a chocolate chip!) and one bucktooth. Dale has a big red nose and two gap teeth.

Goofy

Beloved by most of his friends, Goofy is fun-loving, well-intentioned, and . . . yes, goofy. Goofy has his own way of doing things, which means he often finds himself in comical, if awkward, predicaments. He is also a bit of a klutz, always tripping over his own feet. But never fear. Goofy easily bounces back from even the wildest of situations without a scratch.

did you **know?**

- **Goofy's first appearance was in the film _Mickey's Revue_.**

- **Goofy was originally named Dippy Dawg.**

- **Goofy's catchphrases are "Gawrsh!" and "A-hyuck!"**

Gladstone Gander

Gladstone Gander is Donald Duck's snobbish, lazy, and unbelievably lucky cousin. He and Donald frequently compete for the affection of Daisy Duck. Gladstone is a snappy dresser with a fondness for bow ties and spats, and his feathers are always perfectly curled.

Horace Horsecollar

Best known for his most distinctive vocal characteristic, his whinnying and infectious horselaugh, Horace Horsecollar started out in Mickey Mouse shorts as an actual barnyard horse. But Mickey needed a friend, and Horace soon evolved into a speaking animal. Horace is always ready for a laugh and has proven to be a very talented musician. He's been known to play the drums, the cymbals, the trumpet, the trombone, and the French horn. He is also the sometime sweetheart of Clarabelle Cow.

Moana

Sixteen-year-old Moana has always felt drawn to the open ocean. She feels it calling to her and longs to explore the world beyond her island home, Motunui. But the people of Motunui are forbidden to travel past the reef, and as the daughter of the village chief, Moana has to set a good example for the villagers and prepare to one day take over leadership of her tribe. Moana also feels a deep pull to help her people, and when it becomes clear that her island is dying, she takes it upon herself to leave her home to find a way to save Motunui. Moana is spirited and adventurous. When she feels strongly about something, she never gives up. It is this determination that leads Moana to discover her people's true heritage as voyagers and restore the balance of nature to the world.

did you **know?**

- **Moana's name means "ocean" in many Polynesian languages.**

- **The red in Moana's clothing represents her royal heritage as daughter of the chief.**

- **Over forty designs were proposed for Moana's necklace. The final choice represents her ties to both land and sea, with the stars representing her identity as a navigator.**

Maui

As a baby, Maui was thrown into the sea and left for dead. Maui was rescued and raised by the gods, but he has never stopped trying to prove himself worthy to humans. In the past, he did many amazing things for humans, including bringing them fire and raising islands from the sea for them to live on. But Maui is also the reason that Motunui and the surrounding islands are dying. Eager to find bigger and better tasks to perform, Maui stole the heart of Te Fiti, the mother island, causing a darkness to spread that will gradually encompass the whole world. After a disastrous battle, Maui lost both the heart and his magic fishhook and was marooned on a tiny island for a thousand years. His only companion was Mini Maui, a magical tattoo with a mind of its own— that is, until Moana lands on his island and gives him a chance to redeem himself.

did you **know?**

- **The legendary Pacific demigod Maui is seen in different ways by different cultures and is the subject of many fantastic tales. The character of Maui was inspired by a combination of these stories.**

- **In an early draft of the film, Maui had a grandmother named Hina who served as the guard to Lalotai's entrance.**

Pua

Sweet and cute, Pua is a little pig who lives on Motunui. He is Moana's friend and pet. Although he does not speak, Pua does his best to support Moana. He even joins her on her first foray into the open ocean. However, a bad experience with a wave scares Pua off of going into the water again, and he does not accompany Moana on her second journey.

Heihei

Heihei is a silly rooster who lives on Motunui. When he stows away on Moana's boat, he finds himself accidentally along for an adventure. Heihei doesn't speak and continually does ridiculous things, such as walking off the edge of the boat directly into the water. His best skill is pecking . . . but even so, he often pecks the wrong things.

Chief Tui

Chief Tui is Moana's father and leader of the village. He expects Moana to be the next leader and insists that she must turn her back on the sea and focus on learning about her people and her duties. As a young man, Tui also felt the call of the sea. He set sail from Motunui, but when he ran into a storm, his companion was killed. Now, to keep his people from danger, he maintains the restriction on any villagers sailing beyond the reef.

Sina

Sina is Moana's mother. Compassionate and levelheaded, she does her best to support Moana and help her understand Chief Tui's behavior, especially his opinions about the open ocean. It is she who tells Moana about Tui's own experiences with the sea. Sina helps Tui prepare Moana to one day take leadership of the tribe, and she is very proud of the work her daughter is doing to help her people.

Gramma Tala

Moana's grandmother and best friend, Gramma Tala knows all the lore of her island. She keeps Motunui's legends alive by sharing them with the young children of the island. Tala is one of the few islanders left who know that her people used to be wayfinders. She believes the people of Motunui are meant to be voyagers again and encourages Moana to sail, even going so far as to show Moana the cavern full of boats. Tala is a confidante for Moana. She rescues the heart of Te Fiti when Moana drops it as a child and restores it to her so that she may go on her voyage. Tala considers herself "the village crazy lady" and is not concerned with what others think of her. She does things her own way and encourages Moana to listen to her inner voice and do the same.

did you **know?**

- **Gramma Tala was not in the initial script for the movie.**

- **In a song that was written for the movie but not included, it is revealed that Tala gave Moana her name.**

Tamatoa

Tamatoa is a giant crab monster who lives in Lalotai, the realm of the monsters. Egotistical and showy, Tamatoa longs to be more than just a bottom-feeder. He prides himself on his collection of special, valuable items, and covers his shell in shiny objects to make himself look fabulous. Tamatoa is not fond of Maui. The demigod broke off one of his legs in a previous battle, and Tamatoa has been holding a grudge ever since. The only thing he wants more than revenge on Maui is the heart of Te Fiti, a fact Moana uses to her advantage to escape the vicious crab.

The Kakamora

The Kakamora are a group of small bandits who sail on floating islands of flotsam collected from the ocean. These vile creatures wear coconuts over their heads and bodies as armor, on which they draw their faces and expressions. Although they look cute, the Kakamora are actually quite menacing. They seek the heart of Te Fiti and try to take it from Moana by force.

James P. "Sulley" Sullivan

As the son of legendary Scarer Bill Sullivan, James P. Sullivan always knew he wanted to be a Scarer, too. But Sulley wasn't always the hard worker he is today. As a student in Scare School, he was rather lazy, relying solely on his father's good name to get through his classes. But getting kicked out of Scare School taught Sulley his lesson, and he worked hard to make a name for himself in the field. Having risen up from a job in the mailroom, Sulley became Monsters, Inc.'s top Scarer. Like any good monster, Sulley was raised to believe that children are dangerous, but when a little girl slipped into the monster world, everything Sulley knew was turned on its ear. With the help of the girl, Sulley learned that a child's laugh is even more powerful than a scream. These days, Sulley heads up the Laugh Floor at Monsters, Inc.

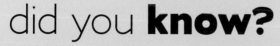

did you **know?**

- In *Monsters, Inc.*, Sulley had 2,320,413 individual hairs. In *Monsters University*, he had almost 5.5 million hairs.

- Sulley weighs almost five hundred pounds.

- Sulley appears in the end credits of *Cars*. He is also in *Tokyo Mater* with a car version of Mike.

Mike Wazowski

As a child, Mike dreamed of being a Scarer. His hero was the great Scarer Frank McCay. Mike even made it into the prestigious Scare School at Monsters University. But Mike didn't have what it took to be a Scarer. He just wasn't scary enough. He *did* end up being a great teacher and motivator. Mike turned that into a job at Monsters, Inc., as a scare coach to his best friend and roommate, Sulley. Mike is a feisty, quick-witted, one-eyed green ball of a monster. As much as Mike loved scaring, he loves a good joke even more—which has turned out to be a good thing. Mike is now the top Laugh Collector at Monsters, Inc.

did you **know?**

- **The original pitch for *Monsters, Inc.* didn't include Mike.**

- **In an early animation test, Mike had no arms and would have picked things up with his feet.**

- **Mike was named by legendary Muppet performer Frank Oz.**

Henry J. Waternoose

A large crab-like monster with multiple eyes, Henry J. Waternoose used to be the CEO of Monsters, Inc. He was the latest in a line of several generations of Waternooses to run the company. This grandfatherly monster was entirely dedicated to the company. He worked as a Scarer for years and personally trained the top monsters working in the business, including his protégé, James P. Sullivan. But today's children aren't easily scared. Waternoose could feel the pressure mounting, and he was desperate to ensure that his family's company survived. Eager to find any way to keep his company afloat, Waternoose partnered with Scarer Randall Boggs to kidnap a young child called Boo. When his plot was revealed, he was arrested by the Child Detection Agency.

Roz

Slow moving, slow talking, but oddly quick-witted, Roz is a slug-like monster who works as the dispatch manager at Monsters, Inc. Roz lives for paperwork, and if there's one thing she can't stand, it is an improperly filed scare report. Mike is a repeat offender, so Roz keeps a watchful eye on him. As it turns out, Roz is actually an undercover agent for the Child Detection Agency. She nabs Waternoose when his plot is revealed and shreds Boo's door so the girl can never enter the monster world again.

George Sanderson

Geor**G**e is a former classmate of Mike and Sulley's at Monsters University and a Scarer at Monsters, Inc. George is a good Scarer, but he's bad at avoiding contact with children. As a result, he is repeatedly taken into the custody of the Child Detection Agency and fully shaved down. Luckily for George, he is a better Laugh Collector than Scarer, and he eventually finds a place on the Laugh Floor, where he can actually interact with children.

Smitty and Needleman

Smitty and Needleman are a pair of maintenance workers on the Scare Floor at Monsters, Inc. Smitty is a green slug-like monster with four arms, while Needleman is a tall, skinny yellow monster with a short tail and a large red nose. The two are constantly quarreling and pushing each other around. Although not a great trait on the Scare Floor, their antics actually work quite well on the Laugh Floor.

The Yeti

Although the Yeti now resides in the Himalayas, he wasn't always a member of the human world. In fact, the Yeti used to work in the mailroom at Monsters, Inc. But the Yeti was unable to follow the cardinal rule of the mailroom: don't mess with the mail or peek into it. As a result, he was banished from the monster world. But this doesn't bother the Yeti. He likes his new life and has even made friends with Bigfoot!

Celia Mae

Celia Mae is the receptionist at Monsters, Inc. Though she does have live snakes for hair, she's no Medusa. Celia is sweet, beautiful, and quite beguiling, particularly to Mike. Things between Mike and Celia were getting pretty serious until Boo's sudden arrival created chaos in their world. Luckily, Celia is very forgiving. Once she learns the truth, she happily reunites with her Googly Bear.

Randall Boggs

A calculating lizard-shaped monster with eight arms and legs and a mouthful of sharp teeth, Randall has the chameleon-like ability to blend into his surroundings. This talent made him the second-best Scarer at Monsters, Inc. But second best wasn't good enough for the ruthlessly ambitious Mr. Boggs. He was willing to do whatever it took to knock Sulley out of the number-one spot—including kidnapping a child and framing Sulley. Randall talks like the slimy monster he is. His voice is raspy, low, almost whisper-like at times, and he makes no bones about hating Sulley. While Sulley is full of modest tranquility, Randall is oozing with hatred and jealousy. Randall was Boo's assigned Scarer. Now, thanks to Mike and Sulley, he won't be scaring anyone anymore.

did you **know?**

- **In earlier drafts, Randall was named both Switt and Ned.**

- **Randall has a nephew named Rex.**

- **Randall squints to see because he isn't wearing his glasses. He prefers not to wear them because when he camouflages himself, his glasses are still visible.**

Boo

Boo—as she is known in the monster world, thanks to Sulley—is an adorable, vivacious little girl who takes her journey through her closet door into the monster world in stride. She is undaunted by the odd landscape and takes an immediate liking to her new friends, Sulley and Mike. Throughout her experience, Boo remains blissfully unaware of the potential danger she is in. While Sulley scrambles to return her home, Boo herself is in no particular hurry. She is having way too much fun! The one thing that does scare Boo is her assigned Scarer, Randall. Luckily, she has Sulley and Mike—or "Kitty" and "Mikewazowski," as she calls them—to keep her safe.

did you **know?**

- **Though it is never said in the film, Boo's real name is Mary.**

- **Boo is two years old.**

- **In an early draft of the film, Sulley befriended an eight-year-old boy named Raymond. This was later changed to the adorable Boo.**

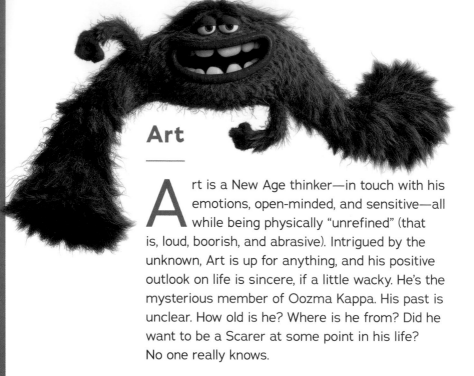

Art

Art is a New Age thinker—in touch with his emotions, open-minded, and sensitive—all while being physically "unrefined" (that is, loud, boorish, and abrasive). Intrigued by the unknown, Art is up for anything, and his positive outlook on life is sincere, if a little wacky. He's the mysterious member of Oozma Kappa. His past is unclear. How old is he? Where is he from? Did he want to be a Scarer at some point in his life? No one really knows.

Terri and Terry Perry

Terri and Terry are classic bickering brothers—well, almost. They share one body but two very different minds. Both Oozma Kappa members dreamed of becoming Scarers their whole lives, but that's where their similarities end. Terri with an "I" is young, naive, open-minded, and a romantic at heart. Terri does his best to fight back against his brother, usually leading to embarrassment and more childish arguments. Terry with a "Y" is a realist who uses sarcasm and humor to hide his insecurities. Like many older brothers, he's easily annoyed by his little brother and loves giving him a hard time.

274

Don Carlton

A "mature" student in his midfifties, Don is a perpetual bachelor. He is the leader of his fraternity, Oozma Kappa. Don is an honest, friendly, hardworking midwesterner, accustomed to a life of sales meetings, with good eye contact and a firm handshake. Having worked his whole life in sales, he's gone back to school to keep up with the ever-changing and mysterious world of "the computers." Don dreamed of being a Scarer in his younger years, but when he didn't make the cut, he realized that was a "silly, unrealistic" dream. But now Don is starting to realize it's never too late to chase your dreams.

Scott "Squishy" Squibbles

A nineteen-year-old college kid looking to define himself, Squishy is undeclared and unattached, and he thinks of himself as generally uninteresting. He's childlike, nonthreatening, trusting, and naive. He shares his emotions easily, be they good or bad. His independence isn't exactly fostered by the fact that he still lives with his loving, doting mother, who feeds him and does his laundry. She also allows him to use their house as home base for his fraternity, Oozma Kappa. Squishy has a way of sneaking up on people that is uncanny, even when he's not trying to scare anyone. Squishy earns his place in the Scaring Program and finally finds himself—he's small, sweet, and SCARY.

Ms. Squibbles

Ms. Squibbles is a single mom raising her nineteen-year-old baby boy. She's a loving and caring mother in her early fifties. Supportive of her son, she's encouraging and accommodating almost to the point of enabling him. She still sees her boy and his adult friends as grade-school kids playing make-believe. Ms. Squibbles is a romantic, and in her free time she is always looking to try new things. Skydiving, dancing, martial arts, improv—you name it, and she'll try it. She has a thing for thrash metal, too; it brings out the monster in her.

"Frightening" Frank McCay

A Scarer at Monsters, Inc., back in the day, this cool, athletic superstar is one of the top Scarers of his time and a hero to little monsters everywhere. A great role model to kids, Frank is always willing to stop what he's doing to pose for a photo or sign a scare card. When it comes to scaring, he's a triple threat: stealthy, quick, and downright terrifying.

Dean Hardscrabble

Dean Hardscrabble isn't just the dean of the Scaring Program; she *is* the Scaring Program. In her mind, there are scary monsters . . . and then there is everyone else. There is only one way to become a Scarer, and it's through her. Students (and even other professors) are terrified of Dean Hardscrabble. She's unapologetically frank. Scaring is dangerous business, and she won't let anyone unqualified sneak through. Hardscrabble is a legend, both as a teacher *and* as a Scarer. She has always been about excellence in scaring. As a professional Scarer, she broke the all-time scare record. And as a dean and professor, she has graduated more top Scarers than anyone else in academia.

did you **know?**

- **Dean Hardscrabble invented the Scare Games and won them four years in a row.**

- **In college, Dean Hardscrabble was a member of the Eta Hiss Hiss sorority.**

- **Dean Hardscrabble keeps the canister that holds her record-breaking scream in her classroom.**

Python Nu Kappa Sorority (The "PNKs")

They may be "pretty in pink," but don't underestimate these young scare students. They'll disarm you with their sweet smiles . . . then rip you to shreds. Smart, coldhearted, and merciless, the PNKs are as mean as mean girls get. Led by Carrie Williams, the PNKs have a way of communicating with each other without uttering a word, a sort of telepathy. Teachers have trouble telling them apart, which they find super annoying. Those aren't skirts they're wearing; that's their fur. In fact, their whole appearance—

including the eyelashes, lip color, and lip warmers—takes no prep whatsoever, since it's all natural. Their eyes also light up in the dark, which comes in really handy when they're trying to find seats in a movie theater.

Jaws Theta Chi Fraternity (The "JOX")

Never seen without their flashy letterman jackets, the members of Jaws Theta Chi are big on brawn but a little short on brainpower. They are proof that just being big doesn't mean a monster has what it takes to be a Scarer. These guys live and breathe sports and scaring. They'll do whatever it takes to win—including cheat, if need be. To their credit, they'll play through pain. The president dislocated his tail

in seven places one year and still competed in the Scare Games. They're not the subtlest when it comes to scaring. Their motto: the loudest, craziest monster wins.

Slugma Slugma Kappa Sorority (The "EEKs")

I f you want to be a member of this sorority, nothing can be more important than scaring. These athletic girls spend most of their days working out and running scare drills. Most of them wear sweatbands on their heads no matter what they're doing, since you never know when you might be able to squeeze in a quick workout. They've trained together so much, it's like they share one brain. They're strong, self-assured, and determined to outwork and out-scare any monster out there. The EEKs don't go home over the winter break; they just stay at school and continue training. Their initiation is a triathlon, and they recently had their dining room converted into a gym.

Eta Hiss Hiss Sorority (The "HSS")

I f you're pale, angry, and sullen and your wardrobe is all black, this intimidating goth sorority is for you. This secret society has been around since the school's beginning, and they are as mysterious as they are terrifying. The HSS are fierce competitors and tough as nails. Rumor is no outsider has ever seen the inside of their house . . . and

emerged alive. Every time they win an event, their president gets another horn piercing. Unexpectedly, when they're not scaring, they perform together as an award-winning a cappella singing group.

Claire Wheeler

The Greek Council president is the emcee of all Scare Games events. Though she's smart and success-oriented on the inside, on the outside she is a very dour, slightly morbid goth kid.

Brock Pearson

A preppy-looking, jock-like meathead, the Greek Council VP assists the president in emceeing the Scare Games. He's loud and enthusiastic, and he relishes the danger of the Scare Games.

Johnny Worthington

Supremely confident, Johnny Worthington is the top scaring student at MU and president of the top scaring fraternity, Roar Omega Roar (ROR). He comes from a long line of MU Scarers and respects the legacy of the school, its traditions, and the system by which it judges excellence. Johnny's big and scary, but smart, too. If he takes a shine to you, he can draw you in with a big smile and a pat on the back—as long as you don't compete with him. If you are the competition, Johnny will use his sense of humor against you, and it's usually mean-spirited, even if you don't realize it at first.

Roar Omega Roar Fraternity (The "RORs")

The best of the best and perennial winners of the Scare Games, Roar Omega Roar is made up of highly elite Scarers. The RORs have won the Scare Games three times in a row, and they are determined to keep up their winning streak. They are ruthless and will do whatever it takes to stay on top. They're a well-oiled machine, and their house is the nicest on campus. Confident, preppy blue bloods, these frat brothers come from families with a long, proud history of scaring. They've been attending scare prep programs all their lives. To get into this fraternity, you have to be the whole package: scary, skilled, and smart.

Mulan

Mulan has always struggled to fit in. She wants to remain true to herself, but finds it a challenge to do so while still bringing her family honor. When her disabled father is ordered to serve in the Imperial army against the Huns, Mulan seizes the opportunity to do something good for her family. Cutting off her hair and disguising herself as a man, Mulan sets off to join the army in her father's place. As a member of the army, Mulan shows incredible bravery in fighting against the Huns. During the battle, however, her lie is revealed and she is released from service. But Mulan is persistent. When she sees a threat coming, she warns her commander, Shang, even though he no longer wishes to speak to her. She also devises a plan to save the Emperor from Shan-Yu, defeating the villain once and for all in the process. When she returns home, Mulan realizes that she has managed to bring her family honor by being true to herself.

did you **know?**

- **Mulan's story is based on the Chinese legend of Hua Mulan, a female warrior described in the folk song "The Ballad of Mulan."**

- **Mulan's name means "magnolia" in Mandarin.**

Mushu

For years Mushu acted as a guardian to the Fa family. But when a member of the family was killed in battle on Mushu's watch, the little dragon was demoted to gong ringer and incense burner. More than anything, Mushu wants to be a guardian for the Fa family again. When Mulan runs away from home, he takes it upon himself to watch over her. He hopes that doing so will allow him to resume his former position. Although Mushu's schemes to help Mulan often go awry, his loyalty to her outweighs his personal agenda. It is this loyalty that eventually earns him back the role of guardian.

Cri-Kee

Cri-Kee is a lucky cricket who may not actually be so lucky. Grandmother Fa gives him to Mulan to bring her luck with the Matchmaker, an encounter that ends in disaster. Cri-Kee then accompanies Mulan when she takes her father's place in the Imperial army. He is deeply loyal to Mulan, and although he is skeptical of Mushu at first, they eventually become good friends.

Li Shang

Li Shang is the son of the great General Li, the leader of the Imperial army. As captain, it is Shang's job to train and lead the new recruits—including Mulan. Shang takes protecting China from the Huns very seriously. He is tough on his troops, leading them through a series of rigorous training exercises. Shang is also very brave—he is prepared to die in the fight against the Huns. Although Shang is angry when he learns that Mulan has deceived him, he gets over his anger for the sake of protecting the country he loves. Shang even helps Mulan defeat Shan-Yu and save the Emperor. Impressed by Mulan's bravery and heroism, he falls in love with her and comes to visit her at the Fa household once the Huns are defeated.

did you **know?**

- **In the Mandarin version of *Mulan*, Shang's name is Xiang, which means "to soar."**

- **Shang was first in his class in regards to military affairs.**

Fa Zhou

Fa Zhou is Mulan's father. He's also "*the* Fa Zhou," a well-known war hero. Fa Zhou has grown older and now walks with a crutch. To him, nothing is more important than family honor. When the Huns invade China, he is willing to serve his country and protect his family again, even though he knows he is unlikely to survive battle.

Grandmother Fa

Grandmother Fa is the oldest member of the Fa family. As such, she has a connection to the Fa ancestors that no one else can share. Grandmother Fa is very knowledgeable about traditions and believes strongly in good luck, as she proves when she gives Mulan a lucky cricket. She has learned that at her age there is no point in holding back and will happily speak her mind to anyone who will listen—and some who would prefer not to!

Shan-Yu

Shan-Yu is the ruthless leader of the Huns. He and his army invade China, burning and pillaging villages along the way to the Emperor's palace. Shan-Yu is a highly skilled warrior and possesses superhuman strength. He is not above killing his enemies in cold blood just to show his strength and is unlikely to show mercy to anyone who stands up to him. Unlike other warriors of his time, Shan-Yu does not underestimate the power of a woman. As far as he is concerned, a warrior is a warrior, whether male or female.

The Emperor

The Emperor rules over China justly and loves all his citizens. He is fearless in the face of danger. When Shan-Yu takes him hostage, he refuses to bow to him. The Emperor is one of the first people to recognize Mulan's bravery. While he will not bow to Shan-Yu, he happily bows to Mulan, showing her respect and honor after she saves him and China.

Oliver

Abandoned as a kitten, Oliver falls in with a street-smart bunch of dogs led by Dodger. Nonthreatening and cuddly, this kitten has strong emotions and, when provoked, will really stand up for himself. He doesn't let Dodger intimidate him. He is persistent when he feels he is owed something and extremely loyal when it comes to his new owner, Jenny, and his friends. Although Oliver enjoys living with the dogs, he prefers his comfortable life at Jenny's house.

did you **know?**

- **Oliver is given his name by Jenny. Before that, he was just called "kitty," "cat," "kid," or (by Tito)** *"gato."*

Dodger

Street-smart and fast on his paws, Dodger is a born leader. This Jack Russell terrier is fearless and devoted once he decides he likes you. He's also easygoing— as long as you don't ruffle his fur. Dodger is Oliver's best friend. That's because Dodger doesn't eat cats. They just have too much fur for his taste! This free, fun-loving dog is one cool canine, and he knows it.

did you **know?**

• **Dodger is voiced by singer Billy Joel.**

Tito

Fast-talking, adventurous, and never shy, Tito knows what he wants and goes after it with a vengeance. This little Chihuahua may be small, but he doesn't act like it. His fiery temper leads him into plenty of fights with bigger dogs, and he's not one to back down. Tito also has a great sense of humor and is a terrific dancer. He loves to clown around but takes romance very seriously. He is particularly interested in romancing Jenny's poodle, Georgette.

Georgette

Georgette is a pampered, spoiled poodle who has no use for Jenny, the gang, or Oliver unless they can do something for her. She really isn't a pet; she's a prize-winning poodle who demands to be the center of attention. In spite of herself, Georgette eventually falls for Tito, whose devotion and dance moves win her over.

Fagin

Devoted to his dogs, Fagin needs them much more than they need him. He'd be lost without this family, who will do anything for him. Unable to stand up for himself, he becomes a victim of Sykes and fear begins to rule him. He even goes so far as to hold Oliver for ransom. But he would never hurt anybody.

Winston

Winston is Jenny's butler, driver, and caretaker when her parents are away. He also cares for her spoiled poodle, Georgette. Patient and calm, Winston is usually the only adult in Jenny's privileged world. He speaks with an English accent and prides himself on being proper.

Sykes

Sykes is usually shown in the shadows, hiding his face like the true villain he is. Sykes does not like being owed anything, especially money. When Fagin is unable to pay back what he owes, Sykes demands that he find a way— or else. Fagin comes up with the plan to kidnap Oliver, but it is Sykes who takes it one step further and decides to kidnap Jenny. Evil inside and out, Sykes is a villainous scoundrel who would hurt and use anybody to get what he wants.

Roscoe and DeSoto

Sykes's brutal Doberman pinschers bully, threaten, and use scare tactics every chance they get. But the two also know how to smooth talk to get what they want. Roscoe is the more coolheaded of the two, while DeSoto is more vicious and even tries to eat Oliver. Luckily for the kitten, the two are ultimately defeated.

Jenny Foxworth

Jenny is the good-natured seven-year-old who falls in love with Oliver. When Oliver wanders into her life, she decides to adopt him and declares that they will be the best of friends. Jenny is rather lonely. Her parents travel all the time and are out of town even for her birthday party. The only adult in Jenny's life is her butler, Winston, and her only friends are Oliver and her spoiled poodle, Georgette.

did you **know?**

• **Jenny lives in New York City. Her address is 1125 Fifth Avenue.**

Ian Lightfoot

Ian Lightfoot is a sweet, soft-spoken elf who has always struggled with confidence. Although he has a loving family, Ian longs for the guidance and companionship of his father who passed away before he was born. On Ian's sixteenth birthday, his life changes forever as he discovers something extraordinary about himself: Ian is a wizard! As he and Barley embark on a once-in-a-lifetime journey, Ian learns to loosen up and starts to see the world for all its messy but wonderful possibilities. And he begins to realize that there's more value in the things he already has than he might have thought.

did you **know?**

- **The film was inspired by the director's relationship with his own brother.**

- **Ian and Barley's pet dragon, Blazey, was based on the director's dog, Carol.**

- **Many of the urban environments in the film are inspired by the city of Los Angeles.**

- **Ian's and Barley's appearances reflect their distinct personalities: Ian is neat and precise, while Barley is messy and casual.**

Barley Lightfoot

Barley Lightfoot is a big and burly nineteen-year-old elf who believes there is still magic in the modern-day world. He is more interested in playing his favorite game, Quests of Yore, or embarking on real quests in his beloved beat-up old van, Guinevere, than in dealing with real-world problems. Fun, loud, devoted, and loyal, Barley will do anything for his friends and family. More than anything else, he loves and encourages his brother, Ian, in ways that are as uplifting as they are irritating. Barley's unique understanding of magic and quests is a very helpful resource once he and Ian embark on an adventure of a lifetime.

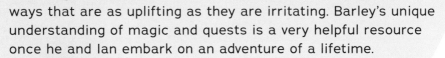

Wilden Lightfoot

Wilden Lightfoot is the father of Barley and Ian. When he got sick, he turned to the ways of the past to try to get more time with his family. Sadly, he passed away before Ian was born, but he had left a magical gift that would provide one last chance to see who his boys grew up to be.

Laurel Lightfoot

Funny, hardworking, and loving, Laurel is a single mother of two boys, Ian and Barley. After the loss of her husband, she focused on providing the best life she could for her boys. Even now that her sons are grown up, Laurel is determined to protect them, no matter how challenging they might make that for her.

The Manticore

The Manticore (part lion, part scorpion, part bat) was once the fiercest and mightiest warrior in the realm. Her beloved tavern was a gathering place for travelers embarking on magical, epic quests. But as modern conveniences lessened the need for such quests, the Manticore's Tavern became a family-friendly restaurant with games, karaoke, and even griffin nuggets for the kids. Now at one thousand years old, the Manticore (better known as Corey) is a practical businesswoman who is more concerned with running her restaurant than reliving her glory days. But she soon discovers there's still a spark of the old Manticore in her, waiting to be reawakened.

Wendy Darling

Wendy can't believe her good fortune at going to Never Land. Peter has been her hero for so long that to meet him and spend time with him is a dream come true. She is fascinated by the mermaids and shows great bravery in the face of Captain Hook's threats. Wendy is flirtatious with Peter and loves the attention he pays her. She doesn't hold a grudge, even against Tinker Bell, who is very jealous of Wendy and Peter's friendship. Wendy plays mother to Peter, the Lost Boys, and her brothers, John and Michael, in Never Land. As much as she doesn't want to grow up, Wendy eventually reaches a point where she is ready to go home and see her own mother.

did you **know?**

- **The original novel** *Peter Pan* **was written by J. M. Barrie. Wendy's name comes from one of J. M. Barrie's friends, Margaret Henley. She called him her "friendy," which came out pronounced "fwendy."**

John Darling

John is polite and very well-spoken. He is smart beyond his years, but he sometimes forgets that he's not as grown-up as he acts and lets his guard down. He is interested in everything and knows many facts. John is particularly interested in pirates and likes to play at being Captain Hook. Adventurous and playful, John also shows himself to be incredibly brave and clever when he comes up against the real Captain Hook.

Michael Darling

Michael is just along for the ride. He gets caught up in the adventure as long as it's not too scary—and as long as he's got his trusty teddy bear. He's even forgotten his real mother. As far as Michael is concerned, he's just another one of the Lost Boys, and Wendy is his mother. When playing with his brother, Michael prefers to act the part of Peter Pan.

George Darling

Full of bluster and fussiness, Mr. Darling needs a good dose of patience to deal with his imaginative children. He thinks Wendy's fascination with Peter Pan is nonsense and that it's time for her to grow up. But he is also a softy at heart and usually feels bad after one of his outbursts.

Mary Darling

Patient and loving, Mary Darling has her hands full with her children and her husband. She is the peacemaker in the family. It is she who insists that Nana will make an excellent nursemaid.

Nana

Nana is the good-natured dog who acts as the nanny for the Darling children. Unfortunately for Nana, Mr. Darling finds the idea of a dog taking care of children ridiculous and decides to tie her up outside for the night. While she's stuck outside, Peter sneaks through the Darlings' window and takes Wendy, John, and Michael to Never Land.

did you **know?**

* **Originally, Nana was going to journey to Never Land alongside the Darling children and have a comical subplot chasing after Tinker Bell. She also would have been the film's narrator.**

Peter Pan

P eter is a cocky, self-assured boy who is as adventurous as he is bad mannered. He likes to give orders, fight battles, and take charge of every situation. The famous "boy who never grows up" thrives on adrenaline and loves to do battle with Captain Hook. It's become quite a game for Peter, who is never afraid. He is followed by his Lost Boys, a group of other little boys who do not want to grow up. Peter loves to listen to Wendy's stories—especially the ones about him. Having never had a mother of his own, he takes Wendy to Never Land so she can be his mother and tell him stories every night.

did you **know?**

- Peter Pan was nominated for the American Film Institute's "100 Years . . . 100 Heroes & Villains" list. Unfortunately, he did not make the final cut.

Cubby

Cubby is the toughest of the Lost Boys. He is heavyset and often speaks as if he does not know much. Cubby wears a bear suit.

Slightly

Slightly is Peter's second-in-command. He is also the oldest—and tallest—of the boys. Slightly wears a fox suit.

Nibs

Nibs is the most active of the Lost Boys. He is also one of the quietest. He wears a rabbit suit.

Tootles

Tootles is the youngest of the Lost Boys. He does not speak at all, instead using a large pad of paper to communicate. Tootles wears a skunk suit.

Tinker Bell

S mart, fast, and capable, Tinker Bell is Peter's sidekick. She is coquettish, pouting, jealous, and spiteful but also caring and protective when it comes to Peter. Tink sends word to the Lost Boys to shoot down the "Wendy Bird" that is on her way to Peter's hideout, and she is later punished for her jealous nature when Peter sends her away. Tricked by Hook, Tink does everything she can to save Peter before it's too late. Tink speaks only in jingles, which the residents of Never Land are able to understand.

did you **know?**

- **In 2010, Tinker Bell was honored with a star on the Hollywood Walk of Fame.**

- **Tinker Bell has become one of the main mascots for The Walt Disney Company and one of its most popular and iconic characters. She has her own spin-off movie series and appears in the opening credits of Disney movies.**

The Raccoon Twins

These two Lost Boys dress as raccoons. They enjoy talking and often finish each other's sentences.

Tiger Lily

Tiger Lily is the Indian Chief's brave daughter. She is loyal to Peter. She refuses to give away his hiding place even when Hook threatens to drown her.

Captain Hook

A true villain who is evil through and through, Captain Hook is obsessed with finding Peter Pan and destroying him. This idea rules his life and begins to affect those closest to him—Mr. Smee, his loyal first mate, and his crew of nasty pirates. The only thing Hook fears is the ticktock of the hungry croc—the crocodile who got a taste of him years ago, when Peter fed Hook's hand to the hungry reptile. Hook never stops dreaming and never stops scheming in his thirst for revenge. And Peter is his ongoing target.

did you **know?**

- **During development, the filmmakers realized audiences would like Hook. As a result, they decided the character would not die in the film.**

- **Captain Hook is ranked twenty-fourth in *Empire* magazine's "50 Best Animated Movie Characters."**

- **Captain Hook was used as a reference during the creation of *The Princess and the Frog*'s Dr. Facilier.**

Mr. Smee

Mr. Smee is Captain Hook's sidekick and puts up with a lot of abuse. He isn't intentionally mean to Peter and the Lost Boys—he's just loyal to Hook. He believes it's his job to do the captain's bidding no matter what. Absentminded, bumbling, and jolly, Smee doesn't seem to realize how bad his deeds or those of the captain really are. Smee may be a pirate, but he has a sense of honor and fair play—warped though it may be. The muddled, befuddled old fellow brings decency—and comedy—to Hook's bloodthirsty crew. When he's not sticking his foot in his mouth, he likes to hum.

The Crocodile

The Crocodile has only one thing on his mind: getting Captain Hook. Many years ago he ate Hook's left hand, and he's been hungry for the rest of the pirate ever since. Luckily for Hook, the Crocodile also ate a clock. Now the reptile makes a loud *ticktock, ticktock*, which gives his target warning that he's coming!

Pinocchio

A living puppet, Pinocchio dreams of becoming a real boy. But to do so, Pinocchio must first prove himself brave, truthful, and unselfish, three things he has great trouble with. Pinocchio has a thirst for adventure and a shaky sense of right and wrong. An easy mark for the practiced con men of the world, Pinocchio often finds himself tempted to take the fun path in life with little thought about whom his actions may hurt. Worse yet, he has a tendency to lie about how he ended up in a predicament rather than tell the truth. Unfortunately for the little wooden puppet, he does not find it easy to hide his lies, as his nose grows longer with each one. But for all his flaws, Pinocchio has a big heart—especially when it comes to his father. Pinocchio loves Geppetto wholeheartedly. It is this love, and Pinocchio's willingness to sacrifice his own life for his father, that ultimately prompts the Blue Fairy to turn him into a real boy.

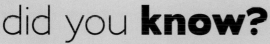

did you **know?**

- **Pinocchio makes a cameo in *Aladdin* when the Genie thinks Aladdin is lying to him.**

- **Pinocchio was made from a pine tree. In fact, his name means "pine seed" in Italian.**

Figaro

Figaro is used to having Geppetto's love and attention to himself and does not always take well to Geppetto's giving Pinocchio attention instead. This feisty kitten has a destructive streak that comes out when he is annoyed. But Figaro also has a conscience and usually feels bad about his misdeeds, often going out of his way to make up for them.

Cleo

Cleo is Geppetto's pet goldfish. She has an expressive personality and shares a close friendship with Figaro, the kitten. They have a brother/sister relationship, with the feistier Figaro showing impatience and disgust at having to kiss Cleo good night. Cleo displays her happiness by doing flips in and out of her fishbowl and shows her unhappiness by swimming around in circles.

Geppetto

A kindly old wood-carver, Geppetto lives alone, with only the companionship of his pet fish, Cleo, and his kitten, Figaro. Geppetto spends his days creating wooden clocks, music boxes, and puppets for children. Although he enjoys his work, Geppetto is lonely. More than anything, he wants a child. His wish is granted by the Blue Fairy, who brings his favorite puppet, Pinocchio, to life as a reward for the amount of joy Geppetto has brought into others' lives. Geppetto is a loving father. He is dedicated to Pinocchio and thinks his son can do no wrong. Geppetto would do anything for his son, including risking his own life to find Pinocchio when the puppet goes missing.

did you **know?**

- **Animator Art Babbitt, who drew such characters as Goofy and the Queen from *Snow White and the Seven Dwarfs*, once noted that Geppetto was one of his favorite characters to animate.**

Honest John

Honest John (aka J. Worthington Foulfellow) is an incredibly cunning fox. Honest John is out for number one—himself. He will do anything to make a quick dollar. Luckily for the fox—and unluckily for Pinocchio—he is also a fast-talker, able to convince people to do things they ordinarily would not. It is Honest John who convinces Pinocchio to go see Stromboli, and who later sends the wooden puppet on his way to Pleasure Island.

Gideon

Honest John's feline companion, Gideon, delights in leading Pinocchio down the wrong path. Gideon seems rather slow-witted. He does as he is told by Honest John, taking his cues from the fox and enjoying his share of the profits from their schemes. Gideon tends to rely more on brute force than persuasiveness, but it works for him and he usually achieves what he sets out to do.

Jiminy Cricket

Jiminy may be small, but he's far from your average cricket. He can turn an umbrella into a parachute and looks great in a top hat. He also possesses a nearly inexhaustible supply of good old-fashioned common sense. It's no wonder he is chosen by the Blue Fairy to be Pinocchio's "official" conscience. Only after he blushingly agrees to his appointment does he realize what a job he's gotten himself into. Like any conscience, Jiminy is occasionally late on the job and frequently ignored when he is around. Fortunately, Jiminy is nothing if not persistent, and he generally succeeds in steering Pinocchio back to the right path— even if it takes a few missteps to do so.

did you **know?**

- **Jiminy Cricket appears in the Mickey Mouse film *Mickey's Christmas Carol* as the Ghost of Christmas Past.**

- **Jiminy's full title is Lord High Keeper of the Knowledge of Right and Wrong, Counselor in Moments of Temptation, and Guide Along the Straight and Narrow Path.**

Stromboli

This heartless showman burns his puppets for firewood when they've grown too old to perform. Money is the puppeteer's sole passion, and his marionettes are only a means to an end. When Stromboli realizes the carnival potential of Pinocchio—a puppet who can sing and dance without strings—he stops at nothing to possess him. Stromboli even goes so far as to lock up the puppet to ensure that his "little wooden gold mine" keeps performing for him, whether Pinocchio likes it or not.

Lampwick

A scrappy little redheaded boy who steers Pinocchio to Pleasure Island, the street-smart, tough-talking urchin proves to be as gullible as Pinocchio. At first, Lampwick is a lot of fun to hang out with around the pool table. But like Pinocchio, Lampwick finds himself too tempted by all Pleasure Island has to offer, and he pays the price when he sprouts long ears and transforms into a donkey.

The Blue Fairy

The Blue Fairy comes down from the stars, transforming from a bright light into a glowing, beautiful woman. Having watched Geppetto for many years, she rewards him for his good deeds by giving life to Pinocchio. The Blue Fairy is fair and compassionate and has great faith in the little wooden boy, even when he doesn't seem to deserve it. She appoints Jiminy to be Pinocchio's conscience until he develops his own, and she keeps a close eye on the puppet. Although patient and kind, the Blue Fairy does not hesitate to show her displeasure when Pinocchio makes the wrong decision. When Pinocchio proves himself by saving the life of Geppetto, she fulfills her promise to turn him into a real boy.

did you **know?**

- **The Blue Fairy's name was inspired by the teal hair of the character in the original novel *Pinocchio* by Carlo Collodi.**

- **The Blue Fairy's appearance was based on the same model who served as inspiration for Snow White.**

- **The Blue Fairy was animated using footage of a live-action model as reference.**

Monstro

A vicious creature, this giant whale likes to eat—and does *not* like to let his food get away from him! Monstro is just how he sounds: monstrous. He is able to swallow whole ships in one gulp and is particularly fond of tuna. Monstro swallows Geppetto when the wood-carver is out looking for Pinocchio, and he later swallows Pinocchio, as well. But this huge animal has a soft spot: he is ticklish. Pinocchio uses this to his advantage to make the whale sneeze and spit out him and his father. Monstro does not take their escape well and goes into a rage that nearly kills the two.

did you **know?**

- **Monstro's appearance was inspired by both a sperm whale and a blue whale. He has the teeth and body shape of a sperm whale, but his size, color, and underbelly look to be based on the blue whale.**

Pocahontas

The daughter of Chief Powhatan, Pocahontas believes in listening to her heart and following her own path. When her father tells her that she is to marry Kocoum, she refuses. She doesn't believe that marrying the brave warrior is the right path for her. Pocahontas communes with nature—often taking advice from the wise Grandmother Willow—and enjoys spending time with her animal friends Meeko and Flit. She is free-spirited and curious, always wanting to know what's around the river bend. When she meets the English settler John Smith, Pocahontas is curious about his world, as he is about hers. She teaches him about the beauty and importance of nature, and soon finds herself falling in love with the foreigner. Pocahontas bravely throws herself in front of John Smith to prevent her father from executing him. Her selfless cry for peace stops a war between the settlers and her tribe.

did you **know?**

- **Pocahontas is part of the Powhatan tribe of Virginia. She is the only Disney Princess to be based on a real person.**

Meeko

Meeko is Pocahontas's mischievous raccoon friend. He can often be found looking for food, which frequently gets him in trouble. He especially loves John Smith's biscuits!

Flit

Flit is Pocahontas's ruby-throated hummingbird friend. He is very stubborn. He wants Pocahontas to always be safe. Although he distrusts John Smith at first, Flit eventually warms up to him.

Grandmother Willow

The ancient and wise Grandmother Willow is a talking willow tree. She often gives Pocahontas advice. Despite her age, Grandmother Willow still has plenty of snap left in her vines, and her bark is worse than her bite! No matter what advice she gives, she always has Pocahontas's best interests at heart.

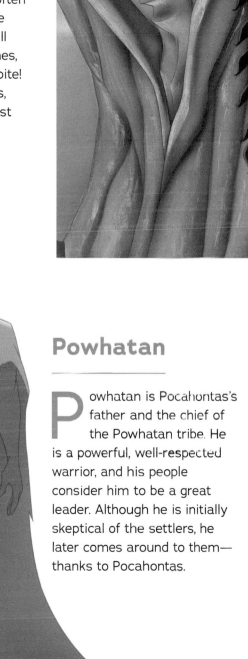

Powhatan

Powhatan is Pocahontas's father and the chief of the Powhatan tribe. He is a powerful, well-respected warrior, and his people consider him to be a great leader. Although he is initially skeptical of the settlers, he later comes around to them—thanks to Pocahontas.

317

John Smith

John Smith is a handsome English soldier who travels with the Virginia Company to help found the colony of Jamestown. He is extremely courageous—on the voyage over, he rescues a young man named Thomas after he falls overboard into the ocean. Due to Smith's past expedition experience, Governor Ratcliffe appoints him captain to make sure everything goes smoothly with the native people. Although Smith is prejudiced toward the Powhatan tribe at first, Pocahontas teaches him about her world, and he is able to see the wisdom of her people. When Ratcliffe fires his gun at Chief Powhatan, John Smith selflessly knocks the chief out of the way, taking a bullet to the shoulder. He is sent back to England to be treated for his injury.

did you **know?**

- **John Smith is based on an actual person. In real life, he became friends with Pocahontas but was not involved in a romantic relationship with her, as he was many years older than she.**

Governor John Ratcliffe

Governor Ratcliffe is the greedy and power-hungry leader of the Jamestown settlers. He wants to find gold more than anything else in the world. When he encounters Chief Powhatan and his tribe, he believes they are hiding gold from him. Ratcliffe is willing to do whatever it takes to find that gold—even if it means war. Although outwardly Ratcliffe is a strong figure, privately he displays great doubt about his abilities. He hides this, ensuring that his inferiors never see his insecurity or have reason to question him.

Percy

Percy is Governor Ratcliffe's pampered pug. Percy lives an extravagant life, spoiled by such luxuries as his own personal tub and a carousel of dog bones. Although he is Ratcliffe's pet, Percy receives most of his attention and care from Ratcliffe's servant, Wiggins. When Ratcliffe returns to England, Percy chooses to remain behind, having become close friends with Pocahontas's animal friends Meeko and Flit.

Tiana

Tiana is a bright, resourceful, enterprising nineteen-year-old who has big dreams of one day opening her very own New Orleans restaurant. Inspired by her late father, she knows everything about cooking and running a business, but she still faces enormous obstacles. She works multiple waitressing jobs, saving every penny (with no time for romance or any kind of social life), determined to overcome all trials and tribulations and see her dream come true. It is only when she is accidentally turned into a frog that Tiana learns that love is as important as hard work. Later, as a princess, Tiana lives with her husband, Prince Naveen, and runs her very own restaurant, Tiana's Palace.

did you **know?**

- **Tiana is left-handed.**
- **Tiana is one of two Disney princesses to transform in her film. The other is Ariel from *The Little Mermaid*.**

Eudora

Eudora is Tiana's nurturing mom, who worries that her only daughter is working so hard to realize her dream, she is missing out on some of the most important things life has to offer. Eudora has been a seamstress for many years and has made Charlotte's continuing array of princess dresses since Charlotte was little. Eudora's family may not be wealthy like the LaBouffs, but there is no lack of love for Tiana.

James

James is Tiana's father, who dreamed of one day opening his own restaurant and who inspired that dream in little Tiana. He imparted to her his philosophy of food—that it brings people together and puts smiles on their faces. He also shared with Tiana his belief that if you work hard enough, anything is possible. James died in World War I, but his spirit continues strongly in his daughter. James, along with Eudora, provided Tiana a warm, loving family, and he taught Tiana that she should never forget what's really important in life.

Charlotte LaBouff

Tiana's friend since childhood, Charlotte is the spoiled Southern debutante daughter of "Big Daddy" LaBouff, the richest man in all of Louisiana. Since she was four years old, Charlotte has dreamed of one day marrying a prince and becoming a genuine princess. Now eighteen, she sees an opportunity to make her fairy-tale dream come true and is determined to make it happen. But as much as Charlotte longs to see her dream become a reality, she is not willing to do so at the expense of her best friend. Tiana is more important to Charlotte than anyone else, and she willingly sacrifices her own happiness for Tiana's.

Big Daddy

Eli "Big Daddy" LaBouff is Charlotte's father. He's incredibly wealthy, imposing, and powerful, but he is also always ready with a hearty laugh. This jovial fellow indulges the whims of his headstrong daughter. More than anything, Big Daddy loves to spoil Charlotte. He can't help it. Seeing her happy makes him happy. Big Daddy is also very fond of Tiana. He has known her since she was a girl and considers her part of the family.

Prince Naveen

Naveen is the handsome, exotic prince from the country of Maldonia. A jazz fanatic, he's visiting New Orleans to experience firsthand the birthplace of this musical phenomenon. Naveen is a charming, outgoing ladies' man who has a problem with responsibility. Recently cut off by his parents because of his gallivanting ways, he is looking to somehow maintain his lavish lifestyle while avoiding his most dreaded fear—having to work for a living. But through his relationship with Tiana, he grows up considerably and discovers an inner nobility he never knew he had.

did you **know?**

- **Naveen has a younger brother named Ralphie.**
- **Naveen is fluent in French.**

Lawrence

Lawrence is Naveen's stiff, pompous valet. Though he plays the part of Naveen's dutiful manservant, Lawrence is secretly envious of the prince's charm, good looks, and position. Dr. Facilier exploits this envy for all it is worth.

Dr. Facilier

Dr. Facilier is a sinister, charismatic tarot-card reader/voodoo sorcerer who works the French Quarter, luring unsuspecting "marks" into deals in which he gives them whatever they want but always leaves them much worse off than they were before. Known as the "shadow man," because his shadow has a life and personality of its own, Facilier spreads darkness and corruption wherever he goes.

Mama Odie

Mama Odie is a 197-year-old blind voodoo priestess who lives deep in the Louisiana bayou with her "seeing-eye snake," Juju. Mama Odie's home is a houseboat placed high in a tree. She's comically eccentric, yet wise and all-knowing, and she loves making big batches of her magical gumbo, which she concocts in an old bathtub. Mama Odie can see what Tiana needs rather than what she wants, and she gently guides Tiana toward figuring it out for herself.

did you **know?**

- **Although Mama Odie can speak to animals, she is never seen talking with her pet snake.**

Ray

Ray is a lovesick Cajun firefly who's constantly pining for his beloved Evangeline. What Ray doesn't realize is that Evangeline is really the North Star. Warm and easygoing, Ray conveys a lot of positive energy, spreading light and always looking on the bright side of life. He believes in true love and is a loyal friend, even going as far as to give his own life to protect Tiana. Ray is rewarded for his sacrifice by becoming a star that appears in the sky right next to the North Star.

Louis

Louis is an alligator who knows all about jazz, having listened to the great jazz musicians performing on the riverboats passing through the bayou. Louis found a discarded trumpet and taught himself to play. He is now a jazz virtuoso. He helped Tiana and Naveen find their way to each other and back to their human bodies. He now plays lead in the band at Tiana's Palace.

Remy

Rats are no strangers to rejection, but Remy, a rat who longs to be a great chef, has more than the usual obstacles to overcome. His remarkable sense of smell and genius for combining flavors puts him head and shoulders above most human chefs. However, in the rat world, he's resigned to a life of being the "poison sniffer," using his unique talent to pick out the "safe" garbage for his family to eat. When he's not out scrounging around for the few gourmet scraps he can safely get his hands on, he is busy poring over his most prized possession: a battered cookbook by the late, great chef Auguste Gusteau. When circumstances literally drop him in the kitchen of Gusteau's, his idol's world-famous restaurant, Remy finds himself living his dream of cooking in a real kitchen.

did you **know?**

- **Remy has 1,150,070 hairs on his body.**

- **Remy is ranked forty-first in *Empire* magazine's "50 Best Animated Movie Characters."**

- **Remy makes a cameo as a REM-E robot in *WALL·E*.**

Emile

Emile, Remy's "little" brother, is a rat's rat: a little overweight and good-natured, he's a lover of life and all things edible and inedible. He doesn't understand the finer points of his brother's obsession with food, but he is always ready to support Remy on one of his harebrained errands or cheer him up when he's feeling low. His bottomless appetite and appreciation make him the perfect audience for Remy's culinary delights.

Django

Remy's father, Django, is the patriarch of the rat clan. Django expects his oldest son, Remy, to one day take over the responsibilities of leading and providing for the extended rat family. He is frustrated by his son's finickiness and reluctance to eat perfectly good garbage. To Django, it's clear that "humans equal death" and that a restaurant kitchen is no place for Remy to be hanging around, not to mention cooking in.

Auguste Gusteau

The late Auguste Gusteau, France's greatest all-time culinary genius, is the author of *Anyone Can Cook!*, the cookbook that inspired Remy to dream of becoming a chef. Gusteau died mysteriously soon after his restaurant was downgraded from five stars to four stars by food critic Anton Ego, but his spirit lives on in his recipes and in Remy's imagination: the great chef is a recurring figure as Remy's imaginary soul mate and counselor.

Colette

Colette is the toughest chef and the only woman in the kitchen at Gusteau's. Her grit, talent, and intimidating air have taken her far, but years of climbing the ladder in the male-dominated world of haute cuisine have made her wary and self-contained. At first, she is exasperated at being assigned to "babysit" Linguini as he begins his trial period as a chef. But as time passes, Linguini's vulnerability and innocence begin to win her over.

Alfredo Linguini

L inguini, a timid and well-meaning young man, is the new garbage boy at Gusteau's. After a series of ill-fated jobs, Linguini is desperate to hold on to this one, which he sees as his last hope. A chance encounter with Remy thrusts Linguini into a highly unusual "ghost-cooking" relationship in which Linguini provides the gangly brawn for Remy's culinary brains. As Remy's food attracts more and more attention, the pair is subjected to increasingly intense scrutiny. For Linguini, the opportunity to spend time around his new mentor, Colette, makes all the stress manageable . . . barely. It turns out there is more to Linguini than meets the eye. Unknown even to him, he is the son of the late Auguste Gusteau and the true owner of Gusteau's.

did you **know?**

- **Linguini's name is based on Italian food. Alfredo is a type of cream sauce used in pasta dishes, and linguini is a type of pasta.**

- **Linguini wears *The Incredibles* underwear.**

Skinner

Skinner, whose modest physical stature belies a domineering personality, is the chef in charge at Gusteau's. Once the sous-chef to Gusteau himself, Skinner assumed control of the restaurant and business when the great chef died without an heir. He does not like to be questioned and will stop at nothing to make sure he stays in charge of the restaurant.

Anton Ego

Anton Ego, the most powerful food critic in Paris, can make or break a restaurant with a single review. The sight of his colorless, unsmiling face strikes fear into the hearts of even the most successful of culinary celebrities. Chefs have become so afraid of displeasing the "Grim Eater," as he is commonly known, that no one dares to change a menu without his blessing. Ego has grown accustomed to this power over the years and by now regards it as his due.

Bernard

Timid yet polite, Bernard is a round young mouse who works as a janitor for the Rescue Aid Society. When Bernard finds an SOS note inside a bottle, he sets off on a whirlwind adventure with a Hungarian agent named Miss Bianca to find a missing girl by the name of Penny. Their success leads to Bernard's appointment as an agent in the Rescue Aid Society. Bernard is nervous and superstitious, but he has a strong moral compass and gains courage from Bianca. He is also physcially strong, often performing feats of strength seemingly impossible for an animal of his size. Bernard lives by the Rescuers' pledge: "Through storm and rain and dark of night, never fail to do what's right."

did you **know?**

- **Bernard suffers from triskaidekaphobia, or fear of the number 13.**

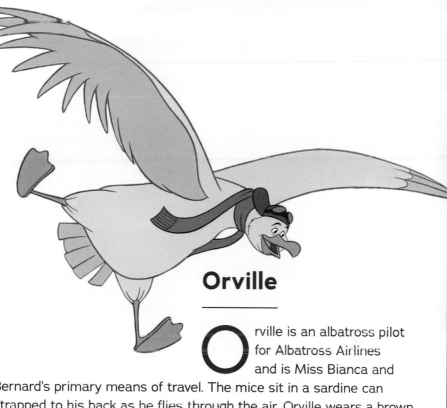

Orville

O
rville is an albatross pilot
for Albatross Airlines
and is Miss Bianca and
Bernard's primary means of travel. The mice sit in a sardine can
strapped to his back as he flies through the air. Orville wears a brown
helmet, pilot goggles, and a lavender scarf, and likes to sing as he flies.
He's not great at takeoffs or landings, but he says he's fit as a fiddle.

Rufus

R
ufus is an elderly cat who's
too old to chase mice. He is
kind and warm and comforts
the orphan Penny when she is sad
that she wasn't adopted. Rufus
helps Penny keep her head up and
believe that one day her situation will
change. Rufus does not think that two
little mice can find Penny, but he is
willing to help them anyway, offering
up whatever information he has
about the girl.

Miss Bianca

Miss Bianca is a graceful Hungarian mouse who is an agent in the Rescue Aid Society in New York City. Bianca is always impeccably dressed in a fashionable hat and shawl with a bow, and can often be seen powdering her face or reapplying perfume. In spite of her attention to her own appearance, Bianca is able to look past the appearances of others. She decides to take Bernard along with her on her mission, even though he's just a janitor. Miss Bianca is kind and compassionate. She is also fearless and daring, and she loves a good adventure.

did you **know?**

- **Bianca's name comes from the Italian word *bianco*, meaning "white."**

- **The decision to make Bianca of Hungarian descent came about because her voice actress, Eva Gabor, was born in Hungary.**

Evinrude

The dragonfly Evinrude owns the fastest boat in Devil's Bayou. He helps Bianca and Bernard save Penny by taking them to Madame Medusa's hideout and flying to get help. Evinrude is green, with big eyes, a mustache, and an orange nose. He wears a blue sweater.

Nero and Brutus

Mean and ferocious, Nero and Brutus are Madame Medusa's pet crocodiles. They act as prison guards and keep Bianca and Bernard from saving Penny several times. The two are fiercely loyal to Madame Medusa, right up until the moment they realize she has no respect for them. Their hobbies include playing the pipe organ, eating mice, and bullying Madame Medusa's business partner, Snoops.

Madame Medusa

Madame Medusa is a greedy villain who has a fixation on diamonds. In fact, she owns a pawn shop that she uses to buy up as many diamonds as she can. Madame Medusa's biggest ambition is to get her hands on the world's biggest diamond, the Devil's Eye. She even goes so far as to kidnap Penny and force her to retrieve the diamond from the cave where it is hidden. Although intelligent and patient, Madame Medusa is also ill-tempered and unstable. She will stop at nothing to get what she wants.

did you **know?**

- **Madame Medusa lives in a half-sunken steamboat. In an early draft of the script, she lived in a run-down mansion.**

- **Madame Medusa gets her name from the Greek mythological creature who could turn a person to stone with just the power of her gaze.**

Snoops

Snoops is Madame Medusa's bumbling sidekick and business partner. He hopes to share some of Madame Medusa's treasure but keeps letting Penny escape. He's a cowardly, greedy, round, balding man with a very thin mustache and a yellow suit.

Penny

Penny, the little orphan who is kidnapped by Madame Medusa, is small enough to fit into the cave that holds the Devil's Eye diamond and has no family who will notice that she's missing. But she's not the kind of child who's just going to accept her fate. She tries to escape multiple times, and when that doesn't work, she sends a plea for help in a message in a bottle. Penny is sweet and affectionate, but that doesn't mean she's afraid to speak her mind. She calls Nero and Brutus "freaky little dragons" to their faces and isn't worried about their sharp teeth and menacing glares. After escaping the Devil's Bayou, she makes national news when she donates the precious jewel to the Smithsonian. Although Penny often expresses concern about not getting adopted, this fear is ultimately unfounded and she finds a family of her own.

Percival McLeach

The cruel poacher Percival McLeach deals in the hides of rare animals and has his eye set on a golden eagle. He's calculating, arrogant, and a bit of a con man: he lies easily and often to get what he wants. Percival dresses in drab, functional clothing and wears the feather of a golden eagle in the band of his safari hat. He is hardly ever seen without his pet monitor lizard, Joanna.

Cody

An eight-year-old boy with the courage of a grown man, Cody befriends the golden eagle Marahute when he saves her from one of McLeach's traps. Unfortunately, Cody is soon caught in a trap himself, but he keeps his cool and saves Marahute's life by refusing to tell McLeach where she is. Cody is a caring and gentle boy but stubborn and strong-willed—traits that come in handy against the vicious poacher.

Robin Hood

Brave, daring, and ready for action, Robin is a master of disguise. He is happiest when he is going up against the villainous Sheriff of Nottingham or Prince John and enjoys his role robbing from the rich and giving to the poor. Robin shows his romantic side whenever he thinks of or sees Maid Marian. Robin is a generous soul who is adored by the people of Nottingham for the way he looks after them.

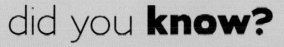

did you **know?**

- **Robin Hood has a price of ten thousand ingots on his head.**

- **Robin Hood appears to be ambidextrous, as he can pull back his bowstring with either hand.**

Maid Marian

Sweet, caring, and head over heels in love with Robin, Maid Marian longs for only one thing—to be married to her sweetheart. Robin and Marian met as children and fell in love as they grew older. But Marian left Nottingham for London, and the two were parted. Marian and Robin Hood are reunited when she returns to Nottingham, but she is unable to fully express her love for him. As the niece of King Richard, she often finds herself in the way of Robin's plans to foil Prince John. Ultimately, however, Marian stands up for Robin and the two marry.

did you **know?**

- **Maid Marian is the only female character in *Robin Hood* to wear shoes. All the others are barefoot.**

Little John

Loyal, humorous, carefree, thoughtful, and courageous, Little John is Robin's best friend and sidekick. He is always looking out for his brave but sometimes foolhardy friend. Unlike Robin, who takes risks, Little John is cautious. He thinks out the potential consequences of his actions and tries to make Robin do the same.

Friar Tuck

Well-meaning and patient, up to a point, the good friar is a man of peace. It is Friar Tuck who distributes the money Robin steals from the rich. He is quite brave and is willing to stand up for his people and what he thinks is right. But even he is capable of losing his temper, as he shows when he beats the sheriff with a stick for stealing from the poor box.

The Sheriff of Nottingham

Big and lumbering, the Sheriff of Nottingham politely goes about his business of looting the poor under the guise of collecting taxes for Prince John. To him, it's all in a day's work. He doesn't see anything wrong with ruthlessly extracting cash from the needy. The sheriff is constantly trying to capture Robin Hood, who foils him at every turn. Although often fooled by Robin Hood, the sheriff is not stupid. He is actually quite intelligent and also rather cheery.

did you **know?**

- The Sheriff of Nottingham was originally written to be a goat. He was later changed to a wolf, as wolves seem more villainous.

Allan-a-Dale

Allan-a-Dale is the narrator of Robin Hood's tale. He is a minstrel and is always seen with his mandolin. Allan-a-Dale shares Robin's story, filling in the audience on what is happening between the scenes. Allan-a-Dale is also one of Robin's men and is instrumental in trapping Sir Hiss during the archery contest.

Skippy Bunny

Skippy is a seven-year-old bunny who lives in Nottingham. He is the oldest boy in his family and can usually be seen with his friend Toby Turtle and his sisters, Sis and Tagalong. Skippy is one of the Sheriff of Nottingham's many victims. The sheriff shows up at Skippy's seventh birthday party and steals the coin he has been given for his birthday. But Skippy's birthday is not all bad. He also gets a visit from his idol, Robin Hood, who gives him a bow and arrow in place of the coin that was stolen.

Prince John

A cowardly villain, Prince John is a weak, pathetic, vain figure who sucks his thumb and calls for his mommy when times are tough. The younger brother of King Richard, Prince John assumes the throne in King Richard's absence. He loves money more than anything and schemes to steal from the people of Nottingham to increase his own treasure trove. Although easily insulted, Prince John is also a bit of a bully. He often picks on Sir Hiss, who takes lots of verbal abuse from this sniveling ruler.

Lady Kluck

Lady Kluck is Maid Marian's lady-in-waiting. She has been with Marian for a long time and often offers her advice about Robin Hood. Lady Kluck is energetic and feisty. She is capable of holding her own in a fight, as she proves when she comes face to face with the sheriff's men.

Princess Aurora

Born into royalty, Princess Aurora is a beautiful, graceful, and sweet young woman. But Aurora did not grow up a princess. As a child, she was cursed by the evil fairy Maleficent. To keep her safe, Aurora's father sent her to the woods. There she was raised as a peasant girl named Briar Rose by the three good fairies Flora, Fauna, and Merryweather. Aurora has a steadfast heart, believes in true love, and longs to find a soul mate. A chance meeting with Prince Phillip in the woods causes her to throw caution to the wind (against the fairies' warnings about strangers). Soon after, she learns the truth of her birth and her peaceful life is plunged into turmoil. Returning to the castle for her sixteenth birthday, Aurora falls victim to Maleficent's curse. By the time Aurora is awakened from her slumber by the prince, she has been transformed from a sheltered girl to a mature young woman.

did you **know?**

- *Aurora* is Latin for "dawn."

- **The running gag where two of the fairies argue about what color Aurora's dress should be, pink or blue, comes from the filmmaker's trouble deciding what color it should be.**

Flora

Dressed in red, Flora is the unofficial leader of the three good fairies. When Aurora was a baby, Flora blessed her with the gift of beauty. It is Flora's idea for the good fairies to disguise themselves as peasants and take the baby Aurora to live in the woods, away from magic. Later, it is Flora who provides Prince Phillip with the Sword of Truth and the Shield of Virtue. Flora's favorite color is pink.

did you **know?**

- **Walt Disney's mother was named Flora.**

- **In an early draft of the script, the good fairies were meant to have connections to nature, with Flora being in charge of plants and vegetation. This subplot was later dropped, as it was too complicated and didn't advance the story.**

Fauna

The nicest and perhaps most absentminded of the three good fairies, Fauna believes in the goodness of everyone, even Maleficent. She thinks that reasoning with the evil fairy will be effective but is met with resistance from the other good fairies. Fauna bestows the gift of music on the young Aurora and raises her to love singing. Fauna wears green and acts as a peacemaker in the fairy household.

Merryweather

Merryweather is a little bit of a downer. She is very opinionated and tells the other fairies that she'd like to turn Maleficent into "a fat old hop toad." She's the shortest, the roundest, and the youngest of the three. It is Merryweather who softens the curse on Aurora, changing the consequence of pricking her finger from death to an eternal slumber that can only be broken by True Love's Kiss. Merryweather dresses all in blue, her favorite color.

Prince Phillip

Prince Phillip believes that tradition should change with the times. Although he is betrothed to the missing Princess Aurora, he prefers to marry for love. Phillip is immediately enchanted by Briar Rose's singing and falls in love with the peasant girl. It is only later that he learns she is the princess he is betrothed to. Prince Phillip is charismatic. He can easily persuade people to agree with him. He's also brave and fearless. He sets off to rescue Aurora from the dreaded Maleficent without a moment's pause and successfully slays the evil fairy to awaken his true love.

King Hubert

King Hubert is a round and jolly king from a neighboring kingdom. He has a quick temper, but he is also quick to forgive. He is good friends with King Stefan and hopes to one day see their two kingdoms joined by the marriage of his son, Phillip, to Stefan's daughter, Aurora. King Hubert likes to eat almost as much as he likes to laugh. He is always holding some sort of food in his hand.

King Stefan

 King Stefan is Aurora's father. He is a forceful ruler and has no patience for evil. His failure to invite Maleficent to Aurora's christening sets into action a series of events leading to Aurora's being cursed. Above all, King Stefan is a loving father. He cares deeply for his daughter and will do anything in his power to make sure she stays safe.

The Queen

The Queen is the loving wife of King Stefan and mother of Princess Aurora. She longs for a child of her own and is overjoyed when at last she gives birth to a beautiful daughter. But the Queen's happiness is short-lived, as her daughter is cursed by Maleficent and she must live the next sixteen years wondering if her daughter is alive and well.

The Raven

Maleficent never goes anywhere without her beloved pet raven. Of all her servants, he is the most competent and the most loyal. The pair share genuine affection for each other, and he has her total trust. But Merryweather turns him into stone, and he will forever stay perched at the top of Maleficent's empty castle.

The Goons

Maleficent's goons are an army of very simpleminded, bumbling creatures who live to follow her orders. However, they are rather unsuccessful at their job. They cannot think for themselves, and when they are ordered to look for Princess Aurora, they spend the next sixteen years looking for a baby. The goons come in all shapes and sizes: some resemble boars, some look like crocodiles, some are tall, and some are very round. They all have grayish skin and wear dark armor.

Maleficent

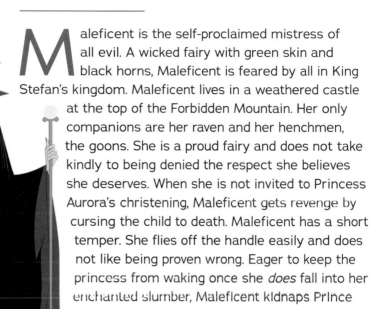

Maleficent is the self-proclaimed mistress of all evil. A wicked fairy with green skin and black horns, Maleficent is feared by all in King Stefan's kingdom. Maleficent lives in a weathered castle at the top of the Forbidden Mountain. Her only companions are her raven and her henchmen, the goons. She is a proud fairy and does not take kindly to being denied the respect she believes she deserves. When she is not invited to Princess Aurora's christening, Maleficent gets revenge by cursing the child to death. Maleficent has a short temper. She flies off the handle easily and does not like being proven wrong. Eager to keep the princess from waking once she *does* fall into her enchanted slumber, Maleficent kidnaps Prince Phillip, even going so far as to turn herself into a dragon to keep him from Aurora. Ultimately, however, her cold heart proves no challenge for true love, and she is slain by the prince.

did you **know?**

- *Maleficent* means "working or productive of harm or evil."

- Maleficent is ranked seventh in *Empire* magazine's "50 Best Animated Movie Characters."

- The sound of the dragon Maleficent breathing fire was created by using a flamethrower.

Snow White

She's been called "the fairest one of all," but Snow White is best known for her kindness to all living things, her motherly nature, and her sweet voice. Ever optimistic, she makes the best of any situation. Even though her wicked stepmother plans to kill her and she is forced to flee the castle, she makes a happy home with her new dwarf friends. Snow White is quick to smile and quick to laugh. Rather than letting Grumpy's attitude toward her get her down, Snow White playfully teases the dwarf until he, too, comes to love her. Snow White dreams of finding love someday, and she isn't shy about sharing this hope with others. The Queen uses this knowledge to her advantage to trick Snow White into eating a poisoned apple. Luckily for Snow White, the apple doesn't kill her. She is woken from her deathly slumber by a charming prince and rides off into the sunset with him.

did you **know?**

- *Snow White and the Seven Dwarfs* **was the first full-length animated film released by Walt Disney Studios.**

- **On June 28, 1987, Snow White was honored with a star on the Hollywood Walk of Fame.**

The Queen

A cruel and ruthless monarch and Snow White's stepmother, the Queen is more preoccupied with being the most beautiful in the land than with governing her subjects. Every day she asks the Magic Mirror who is the fairest in the land, and every day the mirror assures her that it is she. Indeed, the Queen is beautiful, but her expression is sour, and so is her mood. The Queen has been jealous of her stepdaughter's beauty since Snow White was a young girl. When the Magic Mirror tells the Queen that Snow White is more beautiful than she, the Queen flies into a fit of rage. She will do anything to be considered the most beautiful—even murder her stepdaughter. The Queen possesses strong magic, which she uses to disguise herself as the Witch and try to kill Snow White. Although she succeeds in tricking Snow White into eating a poisoned apple, the Witch is chased off a cliff by the Dwarfs. Ironically, as a result of her magic, the Queen dies not as the most beautiful woman in the land, but as the ugliest.

did you **know?**

- **The Queen is ranked tenth among villains on the American Film Institute's "100 Years . . . 100 Heroes & Villains" list.**

- **The Queen never has any screen time with Snow White. It is only when she is disguised as the Witch that the two are seen to interact.**

The Prince

The Prince loves music, and he falls in love with Snow White's voice before he even sees her! They sing a duet upon their first meeting, but they don't get to see each other again until he saves her with Love's First Kiss. The Prince is romantic and handsome. He's tall, with brown hair and blue eyes, and he wears a regal red cape. He also never gives up: even though he only saw Snow White once, he keeps on searching until he finds her again.

did you **know?**

- **The Prince has no official first name.**
- **The Prince was meant to play a larger part in the film, but his role was later diminished.**

The Magic Mirror

The Magic Mirror is housed in an intricate frame. The face inside resembles a dramatic green-and-blue-hued mask with purple lips. The Magic Mirror is a slave to the Queen, compelled to come when she calls and tell her the honest truth—whether she likes it or not.

The Huntsman

The Huntsman is an employee of the Queen. He wears a hunting cap and green and tan clothes that help him blend in when he hunts. Although skilled at his job, the Huntsman finds himself unable to complete a task given to him by the Queen: to take Snow White into the woods and kill her. Seeing the girl talking to some woodland creatures, the Huntsman hesitates in his duties. Rather than follow orders, he warns Snow White to flee and never return to the castle. He then delivers the heart of a pig to the Queen to convince her of Snow White's death.

Dopey

Dopey is the youngest of the Seven Dwarfs. He is playful and eager, with big, protruding ears and a bald head under his purple cap. His green top is way too big for him, and he's always tripping over it. Dopey acts more like a child than the adult he is. Luckily, the other dwarfs don't seem too bothered by his silly antics. Dopey never speaks, but that doesn't mean he can't. Happy says he's just never tried to before.

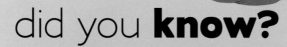

did you **know?**

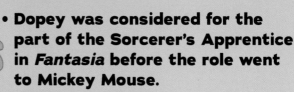

- **Dopey is the only Dwarf without a beard.**

- **Dopey was considered for the part of the Sorcerer's Apprentice in *Fantasia* before the role went to Mickey Mouse.**

Grumpy

As his name implies, Grumpy is . . . well, grumpy. He is a dwarf with a short temper, a large red nose, and a permanent scowl on his face. He wears a red top and a brown hat, and he has a long beard. Despite his disposition, Grumpy has a heart of gold and really does care for Snow White. Other than Snow White, the only thing Grumpy truly has a fondness for is his pipe organ, which he is quite good at playing!

Happy

Happy is by far the friendliest of the Dwarfs, as he shows when he warmly welcomes Snow White to their home. Hearty and cheerful, Happy tends to giggle a lot. He's also known as the singer of the bunch.

Bashful

Bashful, the shyest of the Dwarfs, tends to keep to himself. Any interaction he has may lead to a reddening face, which causes him to hide behind his beard in between giggles. He's a bit of a romantic, and he loves the idea of true love. Bashful wears a green cap and a yellow top, and he has a long beard and a big nose.

Doc

The self-proclaimed leader of the Dwarfs, Doc is intelligent but pompous, and he sometimes stutters. According to Grumpy, Doc sputters like a doodlebug. He also mixes up his words, saying things like "Search every crook and nanny!" But he's still totally in charge. Doc is rational, organized, and kind. Although often at odds with Grumpy, Doc actually gets along quite well with his fellow dwarf.

Sleepy

Sleepy's favorite thing to do is sleep. Always yawning, with dark, drooping circles under his eyes, he seems ready to fall asleep at a moment's notice. As a result, he tends to move a bit slower than the other dwarfs. Sleepy's slow reflexes mean he tends to injure himself often. He just can't get out of his own way in time. But Sleepy is not dim-witted. It is he who understands the animals have come to warn them that Snow White is in danger when the Witch is at their cottage.

Sneezy

Sneezy has constant, severe hay fever, which makes him sneeze a lot. His sneezes are powerful, too; they can blow away anything and anyone. Sneezy's affliction makes it a little difficult for him to hold a conversation. He's a friendly, fun-loving dwarf, and he plays along with Dopey's antics.

Wart

Wart is a twelve-year-old orphan who dreams of becoming a knight. He was found as a baby by the brave knight Sir Ector, who took him in and raised him alongside his son, Kay. Although Kay knows Wart's true name to be Arthur, he finds his younger brother annoying and prefers to call him by his unflattering nickname. Wart is a little bit clumsy but also incredibly hardworking and kind. When Wart accidentally stumbles into Merlin's cottage, everything changes. Merlin decides to take Wart on as a student, subjecting him to a variety of bizarre lessons and even turning him into a sparrow, a squirrel, and a fish. Wart's life is turned upside down again when he pulls a magic sword from a stone. According to legend, whoever is able to remove the sword is the true king of England. Wart becomes the great King Arthur, who, once he gets over his fear of this huge new responsibility, will become a very famous king—at least, according to Merlin.

did you **know?**

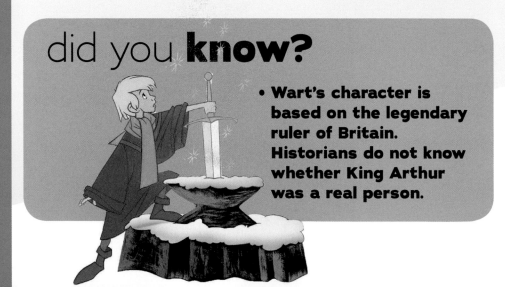

- **Wart's character is based on the legendary ruler of Britain. Historians do not know whether King Arthur was a real person.**

Archimedes

Archimedes is Merlin's pet owl, who has the ability to speak like a human. He's very intelligent and highly educated (he teaches Arthur how to read and write) but also sarcastic, cynical, and grumpy, with a particular distaste for mornings. Archimedes does not mince words. He is brutally honest with Merlin and often points out the wizard's shortcomings. For all his grouchiness, Archimedes cares deeply about Merlin and Wart: he saves their lives on multiple occasions and even tries to help Wart escape his fate of becoming king, before Merlin helps them realize it's not such a bad thing.

Sir Ector

Sir Ector is a pompous, short-tempered, strict knight. He adopted the orphaned Wart and has felt responsible for his safety ever since. He doesn't really show love to Wart, though, treating him more like a servant than a son. Although he cares enough to let Merlin tutor Wart, he makes Merlin and Archimedes live in a crumbling tower that he refers to as the "guest room." Sir Ector hates Merlin's magic. His top priority is helping his biological son, Sir Kay, win a tournament to become the king of England.

Merlin

Merlin is the world's most powerful wizard. He can travel through time and space, he can see the future, and he can turn himself (and others) into any creature imaginable. However, he is a little absentminded and forgetful. Merlin values the philosophy of "brain over brawn" and believes that education is more important than power. This is why he decides to take on Wart as a student. His teaching style is not traditional: for his first lesson, he turns Arthur into a fish. Merlin knows, and teaches Wart, that magic can't solve all problems. This great wizard is tall and skinny with a long white beard and wears a blue robe with matching pointed shoes and hat. When Wart becomes King Arthur, Merlin lives in the castle and works as a royal adviser.

did you **know?**

- **Merlin's magic sometimes takes him too literally. When he angrily said, "Blow me to Bermuda," he accidentally ended up in twentieth-century Bermuda.**

- **Merlin sometimes exclaims "Jehoshaphat!" when he's shocked or surprised. This is the name of the fourth king of Judah.**

Madam Mim

Madam Mim hates all things wholesome, especially sunshine. She is a witch, with powers that rival Merlin's—or at least she says they do. In particular, Madam Mim has a talent for transforming herself into other creatures, including a crocodile, a tiger, an elephant, and a dragon. Madam Mim is not a fan of Merlin's, and finds his rule-following to be tiresome. Dishonest at her core, she prefers to break the rules. She finds delight in the gruesome and grim and refers to herself as the magnificent, marvelous, mad Madam Mim. She looks mad, too: she has a shabby mop of purple hair and huge eyes that are almost hypnotic.

did you **know?**

• **Madam Mim is based on a character of the same name in the book *The Sword in the Stone*, by T. H. White. The author later released an expanded version of the book called *The Once and Future King*, in which Madam Mim does not appear.**

• **Madam Mim was animated by Milt Kahl and Frank Thomas, two of Disney's legendary Nine Old Men.**

Sir Pelinore

Even though they're old friends, Sir Pelinore and Sir Ector are practically opposites of each other. Sir Pelinore is thin, quiet, and friendly and doesn't think Sir Kay would make a very good king. He's also kind; he's the one who stands up for Wart after he pulls the sword from the stone, and he suggests that the angry crowd allow him to try grabbing the sword again. Sir Pelinore wears purple and pink and is slightly balding, though he has a generous mustache. He tends to spill things in that mustache, which sometimes leads to breathing issues.

Sir Kay

Sir Ector's biological son, Sir Kay is slightly dim-witted and totally selfish. He is tall and muscular, with red hair and a permanent scowl on his face. He has tormented Wart his whole life and mistreats him even more when Kay becomes a knight. After Wart pulls the sword from the stone, however, he shows some respect for his adopted brother and remorse for the way he treated him.

Rapunzel

Rapunzel was kidnapped as a baby and raised in a tower, believing Mother Gothel was her real mother. Eager to keep Rapunzel locked up, Mother Gothel taught her to fear the outside world. Despite her upbringing, Rapunzel is down-to-earth, creative, fun-loving, friendly, and brave. She also has magical hair that glows when she sings a special song and can heal any ailment, including old age. For eighteen years, Rapunzel had one dream: to see the lights that rose into the air every year on her birthday. Thanks to Flynn Rider, Rapunzel finally made that dream come true—and learned that she is the kingdom's lost princess. Now it's time for Rapunzel to find a new dream, a task she'll undertake with Flynn and her parents at her side.

did you **know?**

- **Rapunzel's hair is seventy feet long.**
- **Rapunzel's favorite food is hazelnut soup.**

Flynn Rider (Eugene Fitzherbert)

Eugene Fitzherbert grew up in an orphanage, reading tales of the swashbuckling Flynnigan Rider and dreaming of having enough money to do anything he wanted. When he grew up, Eugene changed his name to Flynn Rider and became the kingdom's most notorious thief. Though he's arrogant and untrustworthy, there's no question Flynn can really turn on the charm when he needs to. Unfortunately for him, his charm doesn't work on Rapunzel, and he finds himself leading her into the kingdom—the one place he is trying desperately to avoid. It's only as Flynn gets to know Rapunzel that his true self comes out. Flynn is unflaggingly loyal to Rapunzel. He would do anything for her, and does—literally dying to protect her before Rapunzel's magic brings him back to life. Flynn now lives in the castle with Rapunzel and once again goes by Eugene.

did you **know?**

- **Every time a wanted poster of Flynn is shown, his nose looks different.**

- **Eugene is in his early to midtwenties.**

- **Flynn was originally conceived as a big, burly blond man.**

Pascal

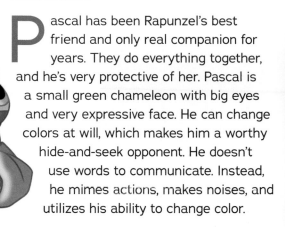

Pascal has been Rapunzel's best friend and only real companion for years. They do everything together, and he's very protective of her. Pascal is a small green chameleon with big eyes and very expressive face. He can change colors at will, which makes him a worthy hide-and-seek opponent. He doesn't use words to communicate. Instead, he mimes actions, makes noises, and utilizes his ability to change color.

Maximus

More capable than any human soldier, Maximus the horse's greatest ambition is to catch wanted criminals. He is determined and tough, stopping at nothing to get his man. Despite his devotion to his job, Max has a soft spot for Rapunzel. He even agrees to wait one day to arrest Flynn so that Rapunzel can see the floating lights. Max also has a soft spot for apples and has been known to overlook the occasional indiscretion in exchange for his favorite treat. Having helped Rapunzel achieve her dream, Max has returned to the kingdom as captain of the guard.

Big Nose

Big Nose is a good-natured pub thug who just wants to find love. As his name implies, Big Nose has an excessively large nose. He knows he may not be the most attractive man around, but he hopes that one day a woman will fall in love with him for his inner beauty.

Atilla

Atilla is a tall, muscular pub thug who wears a vest with leather armor across his chest and a helmet that he never takes off. Although he seems scary, Atilla has a sweet side. He loves to bake, and makes a mean cupcake!

The Stabbington Brothers

Flynn's onetime criminal partners, the Stabbington brothers want nothing more than to kill Flynn and take back the crown he stole from them. They're not very bright and are easily deceived, but they *are* big, dangerous, and mean!

Hook Hand

Hook Hand is one of the many pub thugs who spend their time at the Snuggly Duckling. A large bald man with a thin mustache and a hook on his left hand, Hook Hand carries an axe wherever he goes. But as fearsome as he seems, this pub thug is not all bad. He dreams of one day being a concert pianist!

Mother Gothel

Mother Gothel is the sly villain who raised Rapunzel. She is manipulative, selfish, and excellent at guilt-tripping Rapunzel. She is also incredibly dramatic and vain. Although she seems dedicated to keeping her adopted daughter safe, Mother Gothel's real interest lies in making sure she never loses access to the power of Rapunzel's hair, which keeps her young. Mother Gothel has spent years lying to Rapunzel, but when the truth comes to light, Mother Gothel's world crumbles around her—literally. The power leaves Rapunzel's hair and Mother Gothel ages until she withers away to no more than dust.

did you **know?**

- **Mother Gothel is only referred to by name in the opening of *Tangled*. After that, her name is never mentioned again.**

- **Mother Gothel is several hundred years old, though her exact age is unknown.**

Woody

Woody is a cowboy sheriff doll with a pull-string that, when pulled, proclaims his signature catchphrases from the 1950s TV show *Woody's Roundup*. Woody has always been Andy's favorite toy. Although he was initially nervous that another toy might take his place in Andy's heart, Woody has learned to accept any toy that comes into his boy's room. As far as Woody is concerned, there is nothing more important than being a toy and bringing joy into your owner's heart. Even when Andy is grown—and Woody and friends go to live with Bonnie—Woody maintains the steadfast belief that Andy still cares about his toys. After a series of events that brings Woody out into the real world, he reunites with his old friend, Bo Peep, and joins her as she helps kids and other toys everywhere.

did you **know?**

- **Original drafts of *Toy Story* had Woody as a mean, coldhearted toy. That changed when the animators realized audiences needed to be able to sympathize with Woody.**

- **Woody was originally meant to be a ventriloquist's dummy.**

- **Woody makes cameos in *A Bug's Life*, *Cars*, and *Meet the Robinsons*.**

Buzz Lightyear

A heroic space ranger action figure, complete with a laser beam, karate-chop action, and pop-out wings, Buzz is a kid's dream toy. He quickly becomes a favorite of young Andy, much to the dismay of Woody. But Buzz is no normal toy. In fact, he doesn't even know at first that he is a toy. He firmly believes he is a space ranger stranded on a hostile planet. It is only when he finds himself in the home of Andy's cruel neighbor Sid that Buzz learns the truth and comes to understand how important it is to be a toy. Although Buzz's relationship with Woody gets off to a rocky start, the two ultimately become the best of friends. When Woody eventually leaves to join Bo Peep and her sheep out in the world, Buzz and Woody have a touching goodbye—but know they will always be best friends and will see each other again.

did you **know?**

- **Buzz's fictional home is the planet Morph.**

- **Buzz makes a cameo in *Finding Nemo* as a toy in the dentist's office.**

- **Buzz is 11.43 inches tall without his helmet.**

Rex

Rex may look like the most fearsome dinosaur in the toy box, but this T. rex is one of the most lovable toys of the bunch. Although he's easily scared in general, the one thing that really terrifies Rex is the thought of being replaced or abandoned. Despite his endless worrying and insecurity about his small roar, Rex always comes through for his pals. He approaches life with childlike enthusiasm and is usually up for just about anything—especially if it involves playing a Buzz Lightyear video game.

Hamm

This pink piggy bank with a penchant for one-liners knows everything about everything—or at least that's what he'd like everyone to believe. But there is more to Hamm than meets the eye. He often takes part in the games Andy makes up, playing the role of the fierce villain evil Dr. Porkchop!

Slinky Dog

A dog is a man's best friend—or in this case, a cowboy's best friend. Slinky has an incredible amount of faith in Woody. Although he is friends with all the toys in Andy's room, he is most loyal to Woody. This practical pup will go to almost any lengths to help his friend.

Bo Peep

Bo Peep, a porcelain figurine, was the leader of Andy's little sister's room until Molly outgrew her and gave her away. After serving a stint in an antique store, Bo set out on own with her sheep and her new friend Giggle in tow. But when Woody comes back into her life, she finds herself confronting her past and wondering if there could be more meaning in her future.

Mr. Potato Head

A wisecracking, hotheaded spud with a handy set of angry eyes, Mr. Potato Head is as disgruntled as they come. He's an eternal pessimist with a tough plastic exterior, but his total devotion to his "little sweet potato," Mrs. Potato Head, is as clear as day. Mr. Potato Head is best buds with Hamm. They even team up together in Andy's games, where Mr. Potato Head plays the dreaded One-Eyed Bart.

Mrs. Potato Head

As Mr. Potato Head's biggest fan, Mrs. Potato Head adores her brave spud and is always willing to lend him a hand—or an eye. While Mr. Potato Head's "sweet potato" lives up to her pet name, she also shares her husband's hair-trigger temper. Although she technically belongs to Andy's sister, Molly, Mrs. Potato Head spends most of her time in Andy's room with her husband. She plays the role of One-Eyed Betty in Andy's games, and she also acts as an adoptive mother to the Little Green Aliens.

Andy

Kind and imaginative, Andy is just the kind of kid a toy dreams of being owned by. He loves nothing more than playing with his toys and making up exciting scenarios for them to play out. His favorite toy is Woody the cowboy, although the space ranger Buzz Lightyear comes a close second. Wherever Andy goes, Buzz and Woody go, too. Or at least they used to. As Andy grows up, his bedroom walls, once covered with Sheriff Woody and Buzz Lightyear posters, become plastered with images of sports cars, rock bands, and skateboarders. The grown Andy no longer brings his old toys out from the chest for playtime, but he hasn't been able to bring himself to get rid of them. With some prodding from his mom, Andy recognizes the time has come for him to decide the fate of his favorite toys. But it takes a little push from Woody for Andy to realize it is time for a new generation to enjoy what once made him so happy.

did you **know?**

- Andy lives at 234 Elm Street.

- Andy's full name is Andrew Davis.

- Andy's cell phone number is 555-0112.

The Aliens

O ften heard exclaiming "Oooh!" in unison, the three green multi-eyed squeak-toys came from Pizza Planet, where they resided inside the game with the mighty Claw. The Aliens now revere their adoptive parents, the Potato Heads, instead of the Claw, because Mr. Potato Head saved their lives, and they are eternally grateful. But the Aliens haven't forgotten their time in the Claw machine. They actually picked up some useful tips there and turn out to be quite handy with a different claw when their friends' lives are on the line.

Sarge

S arge leads the Green Army Men, who are masters at reconnaissance. It is their job to keep an eye on Andy during birthdays and Christmas and report back on what gifts he receives. Sarge takes his "no man left behind" policy seriously and will readily jeopardize himself to save any of his men. Unfortunately, his ranks have been depleted over the years, and Sarge knows Andy's departure for college will mean the trash bin for him and his few remaining soldiers. Making what he considers the only possible decision, Sarge and his soldiers choose to make a new home for themselves at Sunnyside Daycare.

Sid

Andy's next-door neighbor Sid loves toys. Or rather, he loves blowing toys up and performing "operations" on his sister's toys to create new mutant toys. Every toy in the neighborhood knows who Sid is, and they all fear him. When Woody and Buzz accidentally end up in Sid's bedroom, they are sure they are done for! But for all Sid's vicious actions toward toys, he may not really be a *bad* kid. He just doesn't know that the toys are alive and he is hurting them. That all changes when Woody makes a plan to rescue himself and Buzz, revealing the truth to Sid in the process. Seeing the walking, talking toys terrifies Sid, and he promises never to hurt another toy again.

did you **know?**

- **Sid makes a cameo in *Toy Story 3* as a garbage collector.**

- **Sid is the only human in the *Toy Story* world who is aware that the toys are alive.**

Mrs. Davis

Andy's mom provides a warm, loving home for her children. But she is not always such a welcome figure with the toys. Mrs. Davis likes order, and she won't hesitate to get rid of things that are no longer of use. Although Woody knows his place in the Davis home is safe, he rightly worries about some of his friends who don't get played with as often. In fact, it is Mrs. Davis who gives away Wheezy the penguin, resulting in Woody's kidnapping by Al, the owner of the local toy store. She also insists that Andy either store his old toys before he goes to college or give them away.

Molly

Andy's younger sister, Molly, was the real owner of many of the toys in Andy's room, including Bo Peep, Barbie, and Mrs. Potato Head. Andy and Molly have a close relationship. Andy helps take care of Molly and even shares a room with her for a period of time. But as Molly grows older, she has less interest in her toys. She'd rather play with her iPod, cell phone, or video games.

Jessie

An exuberant rough-and-tumble cowgirl doll, Jessie's always up for a daring adventure to save critters in need. Jessie is a member of the *Woody's Roundup* gang. She first met the cowboy when he was kidnapped by Al. Back then, Jessie thought going to a museum would be the best thing. She had been abandoned by her previous owner, Emily, and had lost all faith in children. But with Woody's help, Jessie remembers how wonderful it is to be someone's toy, and she happily takes her place in Andy's room. With Andy all grown up, Jessie's fears about being abandoned resurface. Rather than waiting to be left behind, she takes charge, insisting that the toys grab the reins and take control of their own destinies. Although she thinks Sunnyside Daycare is the right place for the toys, she ultimately finds a better home in Bonnie's room.

did you **know?**

- **Jessie is claustrophobic. After spending years in a box after being abandoned by her former owner, she now fears confined spaces.**

- **Jessie makes a cameo in *Monsters, Inc.*, as a toy given to Sulley by Boo.**

The Prospector

Pete, the old prospector, is one of four toys based on the television show *Woody's Roundup*. When he first meets Woody, the Prospector appears kind and grandfatherly. He has spent his life in a toy box and is thrilled to finally be part of a complete set so he can be sent to a toy museum in Japan. But the Prospector is not as kind as he appears on the surface. In reality, his years in the box with no child to love him have made him grow quite bitter. He displays a special hatred toward space-themed toys, as kids preferred them over him. The Prospector thinks that going to the museum will be his salvation, as he will at least get some attention there. The Prospector is determined to see this dream come true and is willing to go to any sneaky, underhanded lengths to make sure it happens.

Bullseye

This toy horse is part of Woody's original vintage Roundup gang. Bullseye is like an excitable puppy, always bouncing around and licking his friends' faces. Although he cannot speak, he conveys his emotions by neighing. Bullseye loves nothing more than a good rodeo. He's fast on his feet and rides like the wind, especially when Woody is in the saddle!

Emperor Zurg

The evil Emperor Zurg is the sworn enemy of the Galactic Alliance and the archenemy of Buzz Lightyear. Zurg rules over Planet Z but has ambitions of conquering the entire galaxy . . . if he can defeat that pesky space ranger. Zurg wears a purple outfit with a black cape and carries a giant blaster. Although menacing, he is no match for the great Buzz Lightyear.

Al McWhiggin

Owner of the toy store Al's Toy Barn, Al is a greedy collector whose goal is to gather a full set of *Woody's Roundup* toys so he can sell them to a museum in Japan. Al gets a chance at achieving his dream when he spies Woody at the Davises' garage sale and steals him. Unfortunately for Al, the other toys see a commercial for his store and put two and two together. They soon rescue Woody and the other toys, putting an end to Al's plot.

Lots-o'-Huggin' Bear

Lots-o'-Huggin' Bear, or Lotso, as he likes to be called, is a strawberry-scented pink plush teddy bear with a kind smile and a pudgy belly. He's the boss at Sunnyside Daycare, and his easygoing homespun manner puts newly donated toys at ease. But there's a dark side to Lotso. He was accidentally left behind by his owner, Daisy, and when he made his way back to her, he found he had been replaced. His resentment toward Daisy has caused him to grow bitter, and he takes his anger out on the other toys. Lotso runs a tight ship. He decides what happens at Sunnyside and won't tolerate anyone questioning his authority. The ones who do cause problems find themselves on a fast track to the city dump.

did you **know?**

- **Lotso makes an appearance in *Up*. He can be seen next to a bed when Carl's house passes by a bedroom window. An advertisement for a Lotso bear can also be seen in Tokyo in *Cars 2*.**

- **In early drafts of the movie, Lotso was a Care Bear.**

Big Baby

Big Baby is just that: a large baby doll. He's adorned with marker tattoos and sports a half-lidded left eye. He serves as Lotso's enforcer and has the simple mind of an infant. Like Lotso, Big Baby was once owned by Daisy, but he was accidentally lost. Years later, his heart still belongs to her.

Twitch

A wrestler with the head of an insect, Twitch lives at Sunnyside Daycare and works for Lotso. It is his job to man the searchlight in the playground, making sure no toys escape from the daycare.

Twitch is also part of the gang that captures Buzz. But Twitch is not a bad guy—he just doesn't know any better. He is eventually convinced that Lotso is not such a good guy and turns his back on the villain.

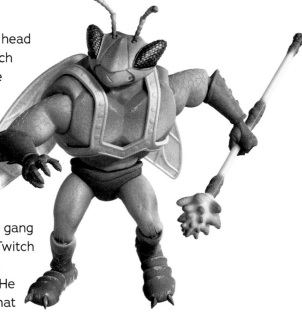

Bonnie

Bonnie is a cute four-year-old girl who attends Sunnyside Daycare, where her mother works. Quiet and shy, she keeps to herself at school. But when she's alone in her bedroom, Bonnie's imagination and personality explode into marathon bouts of energetic playtime. Bonnie is an incredibly loving toy owner. She joyfully welcomes Woody to her room, introducing him to all her toys, and is later thrilled to take ownership of the rest of Andy's toys. On Bonnie's first day of kindergarten, she makes a new toy named Forky using art supplies. He quickly becomes her favorite toy and security blanket as she transitions into being a schoolgirl.

did you **know?**

- **Bonnie lives at 1225 Sycamore Street.**
- **Bonnie's trademark look is a pink tutu.**

Mr. Pricklepants

A stuffed hedgehog who wears a green hat and green lederhosen, Mr. Pricklepants is by far the most dramatic toy in Bonnie's room. He is a thespian at heart and takes his role as an actor in Bonnie's stories incredibly seriously. When Bonnie is not around, he often turns his dramatic flair toward the other toys, trying to rope them into performing one Shakespearean play or another. Mr. Pricklepants knows all about Lotso. It is he who warns Woody that his friends are in danger at Sunnyside.

did you **know?**

- **Mr. Pricklepants is from Germany. He is part of the Waldfreunde collection of toys.**

- **Mr. Pricklepants is a huge fan of horror movies. He's seen tons of them and always knows what's going to happen next.**

Dolly

Dolly is a rag doll with purple hair and an orange dress. Before Woody arrives in Bonnie's room, Dolly is the toy in charge. The other toys happily defer to her when it comes to the running of the room. Dolly has been with Bonnie for a long time. She usually plays the role of the scary witch in Bonnie's games.

Buttercup

Buttercup is a white unicorn with a yellow mane, blue eyes, and a golden horn. Although usually mistaken for a girl because of his appearance, he is not only a boy, but a guy's guy. Buttercup enjoys playing cards and has a rather offbeat sense of humor. Like Hamm, with whom he becomes good friends, Buttercup enjoys cracking jokes, often at the other toys' expense. But he doesn't mean to hurt anyone. He just likes to poke fun at his friends.

Trixie

A blue plastic triceratops, Trixie can often be seen playing on Bonnie's computer. She comes from the same toy line as Rex and becomes fast friends with him when he arrives in Bonnie's room. The two enjoy playing Buzz Lightyear games on the computer together. Although somewhat scatterbrained, Trixie has a big heart and warmly welcomes Andy's toys.

Peas-in-a-Pod

These three plush peas usually reside inside a zippered case that resembles a peapod. But that doesn't mean they have to stay there. In fact, the three are quite fond of bouncing out of their pod and all around Bonnie's room. The peas' names are Peatey, Peatrice, and Peanelope. The three constantly bicker, but what else would you expect from siblings?

Forky

Forky is an adorable and spunky toy who was created by Bonnie at her kindergarten orientation. Forky is filled with self-doubt—believing he is really trash, and not a beloved toy—so he attempts to dive into any garbage can he passes. Eventually, Woody helps Forky realize that he's a valued toy and beloved friend to Bonnie and the rest of the gang.

Gabby Gabby

Gabby Gabby is a doll from the 1950s, so she could be a valuable collectible. But without a working pull-string, no collector will take her home from the antique store she lives in. With her two ventriloquist dummy sidekicks, Gabby Gabby plots to go home with Harmony, the grandchild of the store owner. However, she needs a new pull-string first—so when Woody shows up at the shop, she sees a pathway to her dream of being someone's beloved toy.

Ducky and Bunny

Carnival prizes Ducky and Bunny have always been together—literally. They hang together from the ceiling of a carnival game booth, so they are a little tired of each other's company. But what Ducky and Bunny want more than anything is a kid of their own. They have seen so many toys come and go from their booth, and they hope their turn will come soon. Then one day, they are knocked from their perch by none other than Buzz Lightyear, sending them on a big adventure through the carnival and beyond.

Duke Caboom

A toy version of a daredevil Canadian celebrity of the 1970s, Duke spends his days with other toys hanging out inside a vintage pinball machine at the antique store. But Duke's confidence and swagger belie a deep pain; he never got over his kid giving him away when he wasn't able to perform a stunt as well as the Duke in the commercials.

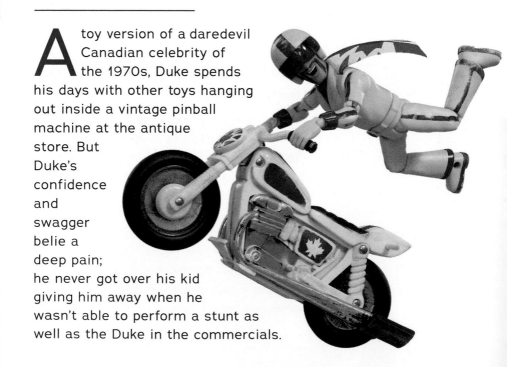

Jim Hawkins

Jim Hawkins is your typical cool, angsty teenager, except for the fact that he's fought space pirates. Jim is very intelligent. He built his own solar surfer when he was just eight years old! Now fifteen, Jim is incredibly guarded and doesn't trust people easily. When he pulls a man from a spaceship crash, he finds himself left with a map to Treasure Planet, which throws him into a galaxy-wide adventure. With the help of his adopted crew, Jim comes out of his shell. As his attitude changes, so does his outfit: he loses his leather jacket, but always keeps his signature ponytail. In the end, Jim returns home to help his mother rebuild and run their inn with the money that his pirate friend, John Silver, gave him.

did you **know?**

- **Jim Hawkins is based on the character from Robert Louis Stevenson's novel *Treasure Island*.**

- **Animators used James Dean as style inspiration for Jim's look.**

B.E.N.

B.E.N., or Bio-Electronic Navigator, is the dysfunctional robot companion of Jim Hawkins. He's missing his primary memory circuit and has faulty wiring, so he acts very glitchy and makes a lot of mistakes. Luckily, one of those mistakes saves Jim's life. B.E.N.'s main goal is to find his missing memory chip, which he does, with Jim's help.

Dr. Doppler

Dr. Delbert Doppler is the notable astronomer who funds the trip to Treasure Planet. He is a good friend of Jim's mother, and he convinces her to allow Jim to go. He's a doglike alien who wears spectacles and a red overcoat. He's very warm and kind, but also easily distracted, especially when Captain Amelia is around.

John Silver

The always-pirate, sometimes-cook John Silver has spent most of his life searching for Treasure Planet. He is a very greedy, very cunning, very large alien with a cybernetic arm, leg, and eye. He's slow to trust, but he and Jim slowly begin to respect, then like each other. Their good will doesn't last, however. Jim learns that John Silver and the crew plan to stage a mutiny once they've reached Treasure Planet, and the two part ways. It's only when John chooses to save Jim's life over getting the treasure he's been chasing that Jim learns how much John values his friendship.

Captain Amelia

The finest captain in this or any galaxy, Captain Amelia is an alien who resembles a cat. She is tall and slim with green eyes and orange hair. She commands attention and respect. She's polite and to-the-point, and she leads her crew with a tough-but-fair philosophy. Despite a fairly rocky start, she finds that she and Dr. Doppler have a lot in common: they are both intelligent, determined, and brave. This, and a life-threatening situation, leads them to develop feelings for each other. The two of them now live back in Dr. Doppler's home, with three children—though Captain Amelia continues to serve in the Interstellar Navy.

Carl Fredricksen

Carl is a shy, reclusive, grouchy seventy-eight-year-old who likes routine and regularity. Each morning he meticulously vacuums every surface and straightens every doily in his home, making sure everything is just as his beloved late wife, Ellie, left it. Carl's life is turned upside down when he learns that his home is being sold and he is being sent to a retirement community. Determined not to lose the one place that ties him to Ellie, Carl tethers helium-filled balloons to his house and takes off to see the one place he always promised Ellie he would take her: Paradise Falls. But Carl is not alone on his journey. He finds an unexpected companion in his neighbor Russell and learns that perhaps it is time to move on with his life, after all.

did you **know?**

- **Carl ties more than ten thousand balloons to his house.**

Ellie Fredricksen

Ellie met Carl when she was a young girl, and the two instantly became best friends. Ellie invited Carl to see her clubhouse—an abandoned house in the neighborhood—and shared with him her dream of visiting Paradise Falls in South America. As they grew up, Ellie and Carl fell in love, and they eventually got married. They even turned their old clubhouse into their new home. Although the two had a happy marriage, they faced many hard times. Through it all, Ellie maintained her sense of adventure and her desire to see Paradise Falls. Sadly, she passed away before they could make the trip. But for Ellie, life with Carl was all the adventure she needed, and she considered her life incredibly well-lived.

Charles F. Muntz

In the early 1930s, rich, clever, and handsome Charles Muntz traveled the globe in his massive self-designed airship, discovering the treasures of the world. For many people, Muntz was a beacon of hope, bringing news of adventure and excitement into their otherwise ordinary lives. When an isolated mesa was discovered in South America, Muntz was the first to go, vowing to bring back something the world had never seen! True to form, he made the discovery of a lifetime: evidence of a twelve-foot-tall flightless bird long thought to be extinct. But the actual bird eluded Muntz, and he spent the next seventy years searching for it, growing more and more frustrated and bitter. Muntz's search for the bird turned into an obsession, and he eventually became a heartless man who could focus only on finding the bird and restoring his reputation to its former glory.

Russell

Russell, Carl Fredricksen's neighbor, is the most prepared eight-year-old Junior Wilderness Explorer in history. He has a GPS-integrated wrist-top personal navigator, high-performance night vision binoculars with a digital camera and long-range scope, a self-cooling and self-heating canteen, and an infrared digital compass with a built-in pedometer. The only problem is that he's never taken his equipment anywhere except the Camping Museum downtown. Everything he knows about nature he learned from books, and he doesn't have any real-life wilderness experience. This hardly dampens his enthusiasm, because he knows once he gets his Assisting the Elderly badge and is promoted to the rank of Senior Wilderness Explorer, his dad will be super proud of him and will pin on his badge at a father/son ceremony. The boy's greatest hope is to reconnect with his father at this ceremony, but to do that he must hound Carl Fredricksen with assistance, even to the ends of the earth and back.

did you **know?**

- **Russell's parents are separated. His father moved out and does not see his son often.**

- **One of Russell's badges has a Pixar symbol, the Luxo Ball, on it.**

Kevin

Kevin is a twelve-foot-tall flightless jungle bird. Although Russell names the bird Kevin, she is actually female. Set free from a trap by Russell—to whom she is forever grateful—she follows him and Carl on their adventure. The explorer Charles Muntz has been looking for Kevin for years, but he has never successfully found the bird—until Russell unwittingly leads Kevin right to Muntz's lair.

Alpha, Beta, and Gamma

Alpha, Beta, and Gamma are the hunting dogs that chase Kevin. When the bird decides to follow Carl and Russell and hide out in Carl's house, Alpha, Beta, and Gamma hunt them down and deliver them to Muntz. Selected for their skill at tracking and smelling, these dogs are fitted with high-tech collars, allowing them to talk. Trained to obey Muntz's every wish, they are intelligent and aggressive. Alpha is a vicious Doberman pinscher and the leader of the pack. He speaks in a high-pitched voice that he hates almost as much as he hates people making fun of his voice. The other dogs follow Alpha's commands without question. Beta, Alpha's lieutenant, is a Rottweiler, and Gamma, his sergeant, is a bulldog.

Dug

Dug is a socially desperate dog who wants nothing more than to be accepted as part of a pack. By virtue of an amazing technological invention, he can verbally communicate with humans. Unfortunately, this talking device doesn't help Dug much in the smarts department, and most of his conversation concerns food, tracking, and squirrels. Dug will do anything to make his master happy—though it's not always clear to him who his master actually *is*. Dug must decide who deserves his loyalty: the pack he's known his entire life, with Charles Muntz—or this new pack with the old man and the little boy.

did you **know?**

- **Dug makes a cameo in *Ratatouille*. When Remy runs through an apartment building, Dug's shadow can be seen on the wall.**

- **The credits for *Up* show Dug with a mate and a giant litter of puppies.**

The Captain

The Captain is the commander of the enormous *Axiom* spaceship, which houses thousands of humans. Trapped in a routine, the Captain longs for a break from the tiresome cycle of his so-called life. His uneventful duties include checking and rechecking the ship's status with Auto, the autopilot. When he is informed that vegetation has been found on Earth, he jumps at the opportunity to finally return to his home planet. On the journey, the Captain discovers his inner calling to become the courageous leader he never could have imagined being and plots a new course for humanity.

Auto

Auto is the *Axiom*'s autopilot. He has piloted the ship for its entire seven hundred years in space. Auto is a carefully programmed robot in the form of the ship's steering wheel, with a manner that is cold, mechanical, and seemingly dutiful to the Captain—that is, until he's put to the test. Unknown to the *Axiom* crew, a hidden mandate exists in Auto's programming: he is never, under any circumstances, to return to Earth. Auto is determined to execute this secret order at any cost, regardless of the consequences for the inhabitants of the *Axiom*.

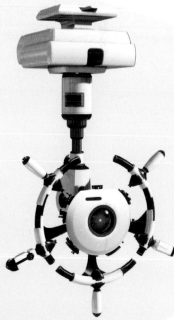

WALL•E

WALL•E (**W**aste **A**llocation **L**oad **L**ifter, **E**arth class) is the last robot left on Earth. He was one of thousands of robots sent by the Buy-n-Large corporation to clean up the planet while humans went on a luxury space cruise. Alone except for the companionship of his pet cockroach, he faithfully compacts cubes of trash every day, uncovering artifacts along the way. There's just one problem. After seven hundred years, he has developed one little glitch: a personality. WALL•E is extremely curious, highly inquisitive, and a little lonely. He has also amassed a treasure trove of knickknacks, which he collects in a transport truck he calls home. His most valued possession is a copy of the 1969 musical *Hello, Dolly!*, which he watches daily. WALL•E's world changes when he spies another robot, EVE, and sets off on an adventure beyond his greatest expectations.

did you **know?**

- **The world around WALL•E was painted in muted colors to make the little robot stand out.**

- **WALL•E makes a cameo in *Your Friend the Rat*, a short that appeared on the *Ratatouille* DVD.**

M-O

M-O (**M**icrobe **O**bliterator) is a cleaner-bot programmed to clean anything that comes aboard the *Axiom* that is deemed a "foreign contaminant." M-O travels speedily around the *Axiom* on his roller ball, cleaning the dirty objects he encounters. His biggest challenge comes on the day WALL·E shows up on the ship. M-O becomes fixated on the filthiest robot he has ever seen. A game of cat and mouse ensues as M-O attempts to wash years of garbage residue off WALL·E. However, even as WALL·E tries to escape this pest, the two eventually become friends, and M-O soon is WALL·E's devoted sidekick.

Gopher

Like most robots aboard the *Axiom*, Gopher has a code emblazoned on his front. In his case, the code reads *GO-4*. Gopher is the *Axiom*'s first mate (or Captain's valet-bot) and secret conspirator with Auto. A roving capsule with a siren light for a head, he is dutiful to a fault. When he learns that vegetation has been discovered on Earth, he does his best to prevent the Captain from getting his hands on it and setting course for his home planet. But Gopher is no match for the persistent WALL·E.

EVE

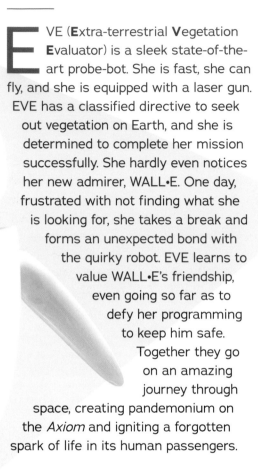

EVE (**E**xtra-terrestrial **V**egetation **E**valuator) is a sleek state-of-the-art probe-bot. She is fast, she can fly, and she is equipped with a laser gun. EVE has a classified directive to seek out vegetation on Earth, and she is determined to complete her mission successfully. She hardly even notices her new admirer, WALL•E. One day, frustrated with not finding what she is looking for, she takes a break and forms an unexpected bond with the quirky robot. EVE learns to value WALL•E's friendship, even going so far as to defy her programming to keep him safe. Together they go on an amazing journey through space, creating pandemonium on the *Axiom* and igniting a forgotten spark of life in its human passengers.

did you **know?**

- **EVE was created with the help of Apple designer Jonathan Ive, who designed the iPod.**

Owl

Owl is a logical sort of owl whose pompous personality makes him seem as if he knows what he is talking about, but in reality, he is usually full of nonsense. Pooh and the others have great respect for Owl's so-called wisdom (as does Owl himself). Owl frequently tells long-winded stories, often about his many relatives and their accomplishments. He can become so wrapped up in his storytelling that he is oblivious to what's happening around him. He can also be a touch impatient at times, but he regards the other inhabitants of the Hundred-Acre Wood fondly and is always ready to help out his friends.

Gopher

Gopher pops up (out of the ground) whenever there is work to be done. His solution for freeing Pooh from being stuck in Rabbit's doorway is to blast him free. Luckily for Pooh, Gopher loses the job for numerous reasons, not the least of which is his refusal to give an estimate! A folksy, busy handyman type, Gopher is also something of a busybody, popping up in the middle of situations and giving unasked-for and often useless advice. Just as quickly as he appears, Gopher usually drops back out of sight down one of his many holes. Because of his large front teeth, Gopher whistles on almost every S in his speech.

Winnie the Pooh

Pooh is a bear of little brain and big tummy. He has a one-track mind when it comes to honey, and he will go to any lengths to get more when he runs out. Pooh and Christopher Robin are great friends who love to spend time together doing nothing. Pooh has a simple sweetness to him that goes beyond the honey stuck to his hands! He is an optimist. Even when things are going wrong, he is still able to see the best in a situation. Luckily for Pooh, he's also rather forgetful, so he often forgets what was wrong to begin with!

did you **know?**

- **Pooh lives in a house with the name "Mr. Sanders" above his door.**

- **On April 11, 2006, Pooh received a star on the Hollywood Walk of Fame.**

- **Christopher Robin received Pooh on his first birthday.**

Piglet

It's not easy being a very small animal in a very big wood. Piglet is little enough to be swept away by a leaf and timid enough to be scared by Pooh's stories of "jagulars." Piglet is one of Pooh's closest friends in the wood. He sometimes stammers when he is frightened and shows incredible enthusiasm for small things . . . like a visit from a good friend. Although often unsure of himself, Piglet is quite agreeable to suggestions from others. He may be small, but he is all heart.

Eeyore

Things are always looking down for Eeyore. With a tail that comes loose and a house that falls down, he's always ready for things to go wrong. Even Eeyore enjoys a good party, though. He proves to be a friend indeed, too, as when he tenaciously (or stubbornly, as a donkey) looks for a new house for Owl. Eeyore speaks in a glum monotone, as if there is an ever-present rain cloud over his head. Eeyore expects the worst out of every situation and finds himself pleasantly surprised when things turn out for the best.

Tigger

Tigger surely is one of a kind in the Hundred-Acre Wood. He's a good bouncing buddy for little Roo, but his springy style bowls over the others. Tigger is always sure of "what tiggers do best" even before he does something. He just as firmly declares that tiggers hate anything he finds that he cannot do or is not to his liking. But perhaps the really "wonderful thing" about Tigger is the bounce he brings to everyone around him. Tigger is shy in front of Kanga (whom he calls "Mrs. Kanga") and often irritates the fussy Rabbit, but his friends love him all the same.

did you **know?**

- Tigger greets people with a cheerful "Hoo-hoo-HOO!" and departs with "T-T-F-N—Ta-ta for now!"

- Tigger has his own theme song, "The Wonderful Thing about Tiggers."

- Tigger explains the spelling of his name as "T, I, double-guh, Rrrrr."

Kanga

K anga is the mom in residence of the Hundred-Acre Wood. She keeps a fond eye on her bouncing baby boy, Roo, and thrills Tigger by calling him "dear." Tigger respects her greatly, and she is the one friend he doesn't bounce on. Kanga often finds herself offering advice to the other residents of the Hundred-Acre Wood.

Roo

R oo is the baby of the group. Fiercely independent, he doesn't always want all the mothering Kanga has to offer—especially when he's ready to romp with Tigger. But at the end of the day, Roo loves nothing more than to go home and be pampered. Roo is polite with a touch of little-boy mischief. His boundless curiosity tends to get him in trouble, but he always learns his lesson.

Rabbit

Rabbit is a practical fellow who likes things neat, orderly, and under control. This is especially true of his garden. Rabbit spends much of his time gardening and harvesting his vegetable crop of "kerits, punkins, and cabeges." Rabbit also likes his house tidy and in order—which isn't always easy with friends like Pooh and Tigger. Sometimes Rabbit takes the time to go ice-skating on the frozen river or off on an exploration with his friends. As long as Rabbit can organize and be the leader, he's happy to be part of any activity. Though friendly, kind, and a good neighbor, Rabbit feels inside that he is slightly superior to the others (though he would never tell anyone that). He often loses patience with Tigger's bouncing and rambunctious ways.

did you **know?**

- **Along with Owl and Gopher, Rabbit is one of the few "real" animals in the Hundred-Acre Wood. The others are stuffed!**

- **Rabbit's first appearance was in *Winnie the Pooh and the Honey Tree*.**

Christopher Robin

Christopher Robin is a little boy and the owner of the toy versions of Pooh and his friends. Christopher Robin is considered to be very wise, and Pooh and his friends always come to him for help. Whether Eeyore has lost his tail or Pooh is stuck in Rabbit's door, Christopher Robin usually has an idea to solve the problem. When things turn out just right, he's always ready to celebrate with a parade or a party.

Lumpy

Lumpy is a little heffalump with a big heart. Although Pooh and his friends initially thought he was a dangerous creature, they soon learned that he was quite kind and harmless. Lumpy's full name is Heffridge Trumpler Brompet Heffalump IV. He is a big fan of honey and bouncing.

Wreck-It Ralph

Ralph is not a hero, but he wishes he were. He works as a Bad Guy in a video game called *Fix-It Felix, Jr.*, and his only job is to wreck things. Ralph is great at wrecking, but that doesn't mean he likes doing it! He is a sweet-natured guy who is just misunderstood. To make matters worse, no matter how hard he tries to do well, he always seems to get into trouble. This could have to do with his programming: he was created to be clumsy and have a short temper. When he sets out to prove that he can be a hero, he meets Vanellope von Schweetz and eventually proves that he's not such a bad guy after all. Later, he travels to the Internet with Vanellope to make sure her *Sugar Rush* game gets fixed. Even though Ralph and Vanellope end up going their separate ways, Ralph was able to prove what a loyal and caring friend he is.

did you **know?**

- **Ralph has been working as the Bad Guy in *Fix-it Felix, Jr.* for thirty years.**

- **Ralph's catchphrase is "I'm gonna wreck it!"**

Gene

Gene is the mayor of Niceland. He's pushy and stubborn, and he doesn't like Bad Guys. However, although Gene initially treats Ralph poorly, he ultimately learns to value him. After all, what are games without the Bad Guys? Gene wears a cardigan over a white shirt and tie. He's short and stout and has a mustache.

Zombie

Zombie is an undead character who is a part of Ralph's support group, Bad-Anon. His body is greenish, he's partially balding, and his sunken eyes are yellow. Although he doesn't speak in full sentences, he still communicates well enough to teach Ralph that labels don't matter and that the most important thing is to love yourself.

Vanellope von Schweetz

Vanellope is a little glitchy. That is, she's a glitch in the game *Sugar Rush* that never should have existed, but she's still the liveliest racer around. At least, she would be if the other racers would let her participate. Vanellope has developed a sharp tongue and a prickly attitude to protect her from the way she's been treated, but she also has a big heart. She doesn't see Ralph as a bad guy, but rather as her own hero. With Ralph's help, Vanellope achieves her dream of racing and learns the truth: she isn't a glitch at all. She was meant to be the star of the game! When *Sugar Rush* eventually breaks down, Vanellope and Ralph travel to the Internet to try to get the game fixed. Vanellope eventually finds her dream game, *Slaughter Race*, and says a heartfelt goodbye to Ralph (although they plan to visit each other).

did you **know?**

- **Vanellope only has four fingers on each hand.**
- **Vanellope's skirt is made of peanut butter cup wrappers.**

King Candy

King Candy used to be Turbo, the star of a popular racing game called *Turbo Time*. When newer, more popular games came into the arcade, Turbo abandoned his game and tried to take over a new one. His actions resulted in both games being unplugged, and leaving one game to live in another has come to be known in the arcade as "going Turbo." The video game characters assumed Turbo was gone, but in reality he remained dormant in Game Central Station for years—until a new racing game was plugged in. He then hijacked the game and took it over under the assumed name of King Candy. King Candy portrays himself as a benevolent ruler, but he actually takes pleasure from the chaos he causes. He's an intelligent schemer and a force to be reckoned with, because he's determined to keep his power through any means necessary.

Taffyta

A skilled *Sugar Rush* racer, Taffyta Muttonfudge is second only to King Candy. She has a huge ego and a mean streak a mile long. Taffyta is the leader of the *Sugar Rush* racers. She and the other racers are incredibly unkind to Vanellope, but secretly, Taffyta is afraid of the glitchy racer—not because she thinks Vanellope can beat her, but because she's afraid that Vanellope's glitch will cause the game to be unplugged. Taffyta is a small blond girl who wears a strawberry on her head.

Fix-It Felix, Jr.

Fix-It Felix is the hero of the game *Fix-It Felix, Jr.* and the ultimate Good Guy: he's charming, warm, and well loved by all. Felix never goes anywhere without his trusty hammer. With it, there's nothing he can't fix. Unlike the other Nicelanders, Felix has never actually been mean to Ralph. He's just never stopped to consider what it might be like to be a Bad Guy: overlooked and rejected. Felix's world is turned on its ear when he follows Ralph into the rest of the video game world and learns just how harsh the world can actually be. For the first time in his life Felix faces scorn and rejection, and he must learn to cope with not always being the guy everyone loves. Felix's adventure makes him a stronger, more well-rounded man. It also introduces him to the love of his life and future wife: Sergeant Calhoun. Together, Felix and Calhoun turn Niceland into a haven for homeless video game characters, even adopting the orphaned *Sugar Rush* racers when that video game breaks down.

did you know?

- In the original script for *Wreck-It Ralph*, Felix was the star of the movie.

- Felix can speak Q*bertese.

Yesss

The head algorithm of BuzzzTube, Yesss is an expert on everything that's trendy and of the moment. She's all about the now, and can even change her hair and outfit at a moment's notice to keep up with ever-changing styles. But Yesss's know-how is not limited to pop culture; she often gives Ralph and Vanellope straightforward advice as they navigate the world of the Internet.

Shank

The leader of a gang in *Slaughter Race*, Shank and her group rule the game with the mission of stopping online players from reaching their goals. Although she's as tough as nails and initially wants to stop Vanellope, the two of them hit it off immediately and form a lasting bond.

Sergeant Calhoun

Tamara Jean Calhoun, the non-playable protagonist in the first-person shooter game *Hero's Duty*, has a tough life. She was programmed with a tragic backstory involving losing her fiancé on her wedding day. To make matters worse, the cy-bugs in her game don't know they're video game characters and will consume anything they find! She's not just fighting for the sake of the game, she's fighting to keep the entire arcade safe. Sergeant Calhoun comes across as pretty tough, but she's not without a soft side: Felix eventually wins her over and convinces her to marry him—after they destroy all the Cy-bugs, of course! She and Felix even end up adopting all the orphaned *Sugar Rush* racers when that video game breaks down.

did you **know?**

- **Sergeant Calhoun's first name is not revealed until the end of *Wreck-It Ralph*.**

- **The role of Sergeant Calhoun was originally written as a man. It was later changed because director Richard Moore felt a male action hero was too boring.**

Surge Protector

Surge Protector is a straitlaced civil servant whose job it is to guard the entrances and exits of the various video games in the arcade. He's prejudiced against Bad Guys and checks them much more often than Good Guys. However, he's got a rebellious side: his hobby is painting graffiti on the walls of Game Central Station!

Mr. Litwak

Stan Litwak is the owner of Litwak's Family Fun Center and Arcade, where all the games live. Litwak's chief goal is to keep his customers happy. If a game malfunctions and can't be fixed, he'll unplug it. The video game characters live in constant fear that Litwak will decide to unplug their games, but it's not his fault. He doesn't know there's another world inside his machines.

Judy Hopps

Judy Hopps is a little bunny with big dreams. A classic overachiever who is passionate about law enforcement and breaking down species barriers, Judy is the first bunny to join Zootopia's police department. She worked hard to get there and is proud to be on the force, although she wishes she were solving crimes instead of handing out parking tickets! Judy gets her chance to do some real police work when she manages to get herself assigned to find the missing Mr. Otterton. Judy is smart, fast, and sly. She easily outwits the sneaky Nick Wilde and convinces him to help her solve the case. Although those around her continue to underestimate her, Judy not only solves her case but helps bring predator and prey together in a way rarely seen in Zootopia's history.

did you **know?**

- **Judy's right foot thumps whenever she is frustrated or upset.**

FREQUENT STOPS

Mr. and Mrs. Hopps

Stu and Bonnie Hopps are warm, loving, supportive parents who don't have a lot of expectations. They don't want Judy to be disappointed or hurt, so they encourage her to have practical aspirations. They are people of the earth: they earn their living by farming carrots in Bunnyburrow and have 276 children. They are generally nervous and cautious by nature, with a particular fear of foxes. Before she leaves for the big city, Mr. and Mrs. Hopps give Judy some fox repellent that they hope will keep her safe from predators.

Gideon Grey

As a child, Gideon Grey firmly believed that predators were more important than prey. He teased Judy for her dream of becoming a police officer and once got in a fight with her, giving her a slash on the cheek that caused a scar she still carries to this day. Now a grown man, Gideon regrets his former behavior. He has become a mature and friendly adult and has even gone into business with Judy's parents. These days Gideon's passion is for baking, not fighting.

Nick Wilde

Nick has experienced contempt his whole life for being a fox; people assumed he was a "sly fox" con artist, so he decided to become one. He's charming, resourceful, and generally dishonest. That's why he and Judy don't get along at first. But Nick's resourcefulness allows him to find creative solutions, a trait that comes in handy when he and Judy team up to find the missing Mr. Otterton. Even though he's cynical and has a completely different opinion of Zootopia than Judy does, the two make a good team. Nick, it turns out, is not all he seems. He is actually quite loyal and empathetic. He's also an excellent actor.

did you **know?**

- **Nick makes a cameo in *Big Hero 6*. His image appears on a billboard in San Fransokyo and on Honey Lemon's cell phone case.**

- **Nick's address is 1955 Cypress Grove Lane.**

- **An early draft of the script showed Nick holding down a job at a restaurant called Chez Cheez.**

Finnick

Nick's business partner, Finnick is a tiny fennec fox with big ears and big eyes who looks like he could be Nick's son. In fact, that is just the role he plays when the two run a con to buy a frozen Jumbo-pop, melt it, and then refreeze it into small pops that they sell for a lot more than what they originally paid. Finnick may be small, but he's more than willing to exploit his size if it means he can make some money. This little guy can be very cute when he wants to be, but his deep voice gives away his age.

Jerry Jumbeaux, Jr.

Jerry is the owner of Jumbeaux's Cafe, an ice cream parlor for elephants and other large animals. He's an ill-tempered, prejudiced elephant who refuses to sell a Jumbo-pop to Nick because he dislikes foxes. Unfortunately for Jerry, his shop also has several health code violations, which makes it easy for Judy to twist his arm to sell to Nick.

Mayor Lionheart

Leodore Lionheart, the fifty-second mayor of Zootopia, is charming, inspiring, and dedicated to keeping the city and its citizens safe—though he sometimes has to break the law to make that happen. Lionheart believes strongly in predator and prey mingling in peace. It is he who hires Judy to be the first-ever bunny cop. He was also the one who coined the phrase "In Zootopia, anyone can be anything."

Clawhauser

Benjamin Clawhauser works the front desk of the Zootopia Police Department. Large and round with a sunny disposition, this cheetah is friendly to everyone he meets. His favorite snack is doughnuts. He's also a huge fan of the pop star Gazelle. Some would call him lazy, but he may just be saving his energy so he can dance up a storm at her next concert!

Assistant Mayor Bellwether

Assistant Mayor Bellwether hides her ruthless nature behind a timid and sweet exterior: the sheep is actually the mastermind behind a scheme to help the "little guys" rise to power in Zootopia. Bellwether comes across as harried and bumbling with her large spectacles and fluffy white wool, and she is constantly talked down to and mistreated by her boss, Mayor Lionheart. However, she is very intelligent and tired of being underestimated. She believes she can unite the prey animals, which make up 90 percent of the population, against all predators, and will go to any length to achieve her goal.

did you **know?**

- **Bellwether's outfit and glasses change in every scene.**
- **Bellwether's first name is Dawn.**

Mr. Otterton

Emmitt Otterton is a mild-mannered and polite otter. But when he is injected with "night howler" serum, this kind otter turns into a savage beast. A family man and a florist, Mr. Otterton has a loving wife and two children. He wears large glasses and a green plaid shirt under a green vest.

Mrs. Otterton

A dedicated wife and mother, Mrs. Otterton is desperate to find out what happened to her husband. She sticks by his side when she sees him in a state of mindless savagery because she knows his true nature. She has a kind face and big green eyes, and she dresses cozily in pastel sweaters.

Chief Bogo

The head of the Zootopia Police Department, Chief Bogo is an unforgiving Cape buffalo. He's very muscular and has gray fur, beige horns that curl upward, and deep-set eyes. He is dedicated to his job, but hates the idea of having a bunny on his force. It's nothing against Judy herself— he just thinks she's too small to do the job. Bogo has a tendency to be spiteful. Annoyed at having been saddled with Judy, he first assigns her to parking duty and later gives her an unreasonably short amount of time to solve a case. However, Judy earns his grudging respect, and the two develop a great working relationship.

did you **know?**

- **Bogo's name comes from the word *mbogo*, which means "Cape buffalo" in Swahili.**

Mr. Big

Mr. Big is a dangerous and useful man to know. A self-made millionaire and crime boss, Mr. Big is a tiny Arctic shrew with a big personality (and huge eyebrows). He values family and is very loyal, though he won't stand for betrayal. Mr. Big has a history with Nick Wilde, but he overlooks it at the request of his daughter, Fru Fru, whom he loves more than life itself.

Fru Fru

Daughter of the crime boss Mr. Big, Fru Fru is a sweet and caring Arctic shrew. She's somewhat spoiled and loves shopping with her father's money. She has a great sense of style and wears her hair teased high above her head. Her favorite article of clothing is a pair of leopard-print jeggings. Fru Fru takes an immediate liking to Judy when the bunny saves her life and is instrumental in helping Judy get the information she needs to solve her case.

Manchas

Mr. Manchas, a jaguar who chauffeurs for Tundratown Limo-Service, doesn't like trouble. He was driving Mr. Otterton when the otter went savage, so he's important to Judy and Nick's investigation. However, his ordeal with Mr. Otterton has made him paranoid and reclusive, and that in turn makes him difficult to get information from. He's also been infected by the night howlers. As a savage beast, Manchas is not one to mess with.

Koslov

A henchman of Mr. Big's, Koslov is a silent but large and menacing polar bear. He mostly communicates in growls. He has bushy eyebrows and dark circles around his eyes.

Yax

A hippie yak, Yax is a very laid-back nudist who believes that animals should return to a more enlightened and natural time. He is mellow and seems slow-witted but has an excellent memory. His hair is in a shaggy style that covers his eyes, and he doesn't like to shower. He wears nothing but groovy jewelry and orange flowers in his hair.

Flash

Flash is the fastest employee at the Department of Mammal Vehicles. Unfortunately for Judy, he is also a sloth, which means his fastest is still pretty slow. Flash has a great, if delayed, sense of humor. He is soft-spoken, professional, and deliberate, but he works too slowly for the impatient Judy.